LUCAS RUBIX

CRYPTO WEALTH

The Underdog Investor's Guide to
**Cryptocurrency, Bitcoin, DeFi,
Yield Farming**, and Creating
Financial Freedom Without Banks

WITHOUT WALL STREET

Crypto Wealth Without Wall Street

Copyright © 2025 by Lucas Rubix

Paperback: 979-8-9937792-0-1
Hardcover: 979-8-9937792-1-8

Published by

The Publishing Pad
www.thepublishingpad.com

Table of Contents

Your Money Is Already Digital (You Just Don't Control It Yet) v

Important Disclaimers: Please Read Before Proceeding. xvii

Part I: The Underdog's Awakening 1

1   The System Is Optional: Why Wall Street
Doesn't Want You Rich. 3

2   Bitcoin 101: The Foundation of a New Financial World 11

3   The Fiat Trap: How Inflation and Banks Steal Your Wealth 19

4   Blockchain Demystified: The Hidden Tech
Changing Everything 27

5   Asymmetric Bets: How Underdogs
Turn Small Stakes into Big Wins. 35

Part II: Crypto Wealth Foundations. 47

6   Your First $100 in Crypto (Without Getting Scammed). 49

7   Permission vs. Freedom: Why Crypto Is the Exit Door 59

8   Not Your Keys, Not Your Coins: How to Actually Own
Your Wealth 67

9   Ethereum and Smart Contracts: The Internet of Money. 75

10 The Digital Wild West: Protecting Your Wealth in Crypto 81

Part III: Market Mastery. 87

11 Market Cycles and Psychology: How the Crowd Creates
Opportunities. 89

12 The HODL Philosophy: Getting Rich by Doing Nothing 97

13 Why Chaos Creates Wealth: Profiting in Uncertainty........ 105

14 Due Diligence Secrets: How to Invest With Confidence,
    Not Guesswork..111

15 Building Wealth Through Portfolio Design, Not Luck 119

16 The Art of Taking Profits Before Greed Becomes Regret 127

Part IV: Becoming Your Own Bank **135**

17 Building Your Own Financial System with DeFi 137

18 DeFi Basics: Yield Farming and Liquidity
    Provision Made Simple....................................145

19 Impermanent Loss Explained (And How to Avoid It)........155

20 The Velocity of Money: Making Crypto Work for You 167

21 Advanced DeFi: Concentrated Liquidity and
    Next-Level Yield...175

22 The Future of DeFi: Where the Financial
    Revolution Is Headed 183

Part V: The Investor Mindset **191**

23 Finding Your Why: The Inner Game of Wealth 193

24 Why Everything Gets Worse Before It Gets Better 203

25 Risk vs. Reward: How Real Investors Think 213

26 Wealth Principles They Don't Teach You In School......... 221

See Ya Out There! 231

About the Author 235

Your Money Is Already Digital (You Just Don't Control It Yet)

Every dollar in your bank account is digital. When you check your balance on your phone, you're looking at numbers in a database. When you swipe your credit card, electrons move between servers. When your employer deposits your paycheck, no physical cash changes hands. Your money has been digital for decades.

There's just one problem: you've never actually controlled it.

The bank controls it. The government monitors it. Payment processors gatekeep it. And every year, they print more of it, making yours worth less.

But what if I told you there's another financial system being built right now, one without gatekeepers? One where you actually own your money. Where no one can freeze your account because they don't like your politics. Where you can earn the yields that banks usually keep for themselves. Where sending money across the world takes seconds, not days, and costs pennies, not hundreds of dollars.

This isn't some distant future. It's happening right now. While you're reading this, millions of people are using this new financial system to invest, build wealth, start businesses, and take control of their financial futures.

Welcome to the fascinating world of crypto. And, if you play it right, welcome to the biggest opportunity of your lifetime.

The Journey That Brought Me Here

Let me tell you about the path that led me to write this book, because if someone like me can make it, so can you.

After high school, college wasn't an option. My family didn't have that kind of money, and taking on massive debt for a degree seemed insane. So I did what kids like me do: I worked random jobs while trying to figure out life. Construction sites, auto parts shops, car washes. Anywhere that would pay me to work with my hands. I loved cars, and I still do, but washing them for minimum wage wasn't building a future.

Then one day, this jacked dude in a yellow Corvette pulled up at the parking lot at the auto parts store I was working at. Beautiful car. My dream car at the time, actually. I had to know.

"What do you do for a living?" I asked.

"Oil rigs," he said.

My brain made a simple equation: Corvette equals oil rigs. Oil rigs equal Corvette. Sign me up.

For six years, I worked those rigs in northern British Columbia and Alberta. Twelve-hour days in −40° weather. The money was really good. Six figures for a kid with no degree. By 24, I had it all: a brand new shiny Jeep (financed), a suburban Vancouver condo (mortgaged), and the external appearance of having "made it." Instagram would've loved me.

The reality? I was dying inside. Gone for weeks at a time, destroying my body in brutal weather, watching relationships fall apart because I was never there. I was making money but losing everything else, including my health, my relationships, and my passion for life. Depression hit hard. The Corvette dream became a nightmare. All my financed toys, mortgaged property, and "vacations" I was booking just to escape reality started feeling more like a prison than the freedom I thought they would bring.

But here's what really ate at me: even making six figures, I was falling behind. Every year, that good salary bought less. Property taxes and condo fees kept climbing. The chiropractor visits for my destroyed back (my thank-you for hard labour) went from $80 to $140 per session. Massage therapy to manage the pain from years of rig work doubled in price. The same basket of groceries that used to cost $100 was now $180. Gas, insurance, flights home to see family, everything was climbing faster than my raises.

I did the math one night and nearly threw up. At my current savings rate, with my "high-yield" 0.5% savings account and 7% inflation, I'd need forty-five years to retire. Forty-five years of frozen hell, and that's if nothing went wrong—no health issues, no job loss, no family emergencies. The "good money" everyone praised me for making was actually a slow-motion trap. Yeah, but no thanks.

My Escape

Eventually, enough was enough. I quit without any plan, just the desperate desire for something better. During all the free time I suddenly had, I became obsessed with a simple question: How do people actually get wealthy? Not rig worker wealth, where you trade your body and time for dollars, but true wealth. The kind where money works for you, and you get back the most precious commodity of all: your time.

As I researched, two themes kept appearing: entrepreneurship and investing.

So I dove in. My first business was personal training. Two years of losses. Lost the Jeep, lost the apartment, watched everything I'd worked so hard for disappear. There were nights I'd drive around in my old beater car I'd downgraded to, stressed about how I was going to pay rent that month, all while keeping a light foot on the gas because I could barely afford to fill the tank as it was. What the hell was I doing with my life?

But something eventually clicked. After two years of failure, I had my first profitable month. Then another. Built that business to six figures, then started another online. That one hit. Made my first million. With that money, I started investing in traditional markets. You know, Wall Street stuff like stocks, index funds, all the "responsible" investments banks push while charging ridiculous fees to "manage" your money. Here's the kicker: they make money off you regardless of how your investments perform. Win or lose, they get paid. After their 2% management fees, plus hidden expense ratios, plus transaction costs, my "solid" 8% returns became 5%. At that rate, my escape velocity was still decades away.

Then in 2020, I discovered crypto. Not as a get-rich-quick scheme, but as a fundamental reimagining of how money could work. Here was a system where your wealth couldn't be frozen, inflated away, or confiscated. Where you could transact with anyone globally without permission. *Where code replaced corruption.* Where you could become the bank.

My early journey was messy. I bought Bitcoin at peaks, panic-sold during dips, lost six figures when Terra Luna collapsed. Invested and lost money in Ponzis and pump-and-dumps. Every mistake you can make, I made. But each failure taught me something valuable. And between those failures, something incredible was happening. I was starting to see a path to building wealth faster than I ever imagined possible.

The Greatest Financial Revolution Hidden in Plain Sight

In 2008, while the global financial system was collapsing and banks were getting trillion-dollar bailouts, an anonymous programmer released a nine-page document that would change everything. The Bitcoin white paper wasn't just proposing new money. It was proposing an entirely new way for humans to transfer value without trusting intermediaries.

For the first time in history, we could send money directly to each other without a bank in the middle. We could store value without trusting a government not to debase it. We could verify every transaction ourselves instead of trusting institutional ledgers.

Fast-forward to today. That little experiment has grown into a multi-trillion-dollar ecosystem. Major corporations hold Bitcoin on their balance sheets. Countries are making it a legal tender. The world's largest investment firms are building crypto products. The smartest developers are leaving Silicon Valley to build in crypto.

But Bitcoin was just the beginning. Ethereum introduced smart contracts, which are basically programs that automatically execute financial agreements. DeFi rebuilt every financial service without banks. Suddenly, instead of accepting 0.05% from a bank that's lending your money at 15%, you could lend directly and earn 8% or more yourself.

I'll never forget my first DeFi transaction. It was a simple transaction, but it's the moment it all clicked for me. I deposited stablecoins into a lending protocol. No application. No credit check. No waiting. I just connected my wallet and started earning 160 times what my bank offered. That's when I knew: we don't need their system anymore.

The Day that Changed Everything for Me

February 2022. The Canadian trucker convoy. You may remember the politics, but what you might not remember is what happened to people's money. The Canadian government froze bank accounts of anyone who donated to causes they opposed. Not criminals. Not terrorists. Regular citizens who'd sent $50 to support the truckers.

I was one of them. I have a soft spot for truckers (and for anyone in the trades). After six years on the rigs, I knew these people. I worked alongside them. These aren't just workers; they're the backbone of civilization. It's truckers who keep groceries stocked in stores so you can feed your family. It's electricians who maintain the power grid so you have lights in your house and heat in the winter. It's road workers who keep highways driveable so you can get where you need to go safely. These people work in brutal conditions, away from their families, keeping society functioning while everyone else takes it for granted.

During the pandemic, while everyone else worked from home in pajamas, these people kept showing up. They were "essential workers" when it was convenient, heroes when we needed them. But the second they stood up for something they believed in? Suddenly they were the enemy. Their bank accounts frozen. Their livelihoods destroyed. Their ability to buy food for their kids eliminated with a keystroke.

When I saw truckers standing up for their beliefs, I recognized them as the same type of hardworking people I'd known on the rigs. I donated to show support for these workers whose struggle I understood firsthand. Then came the announcement: anyone who supported them could have their accounts frozen.

Think about that. Every dollar I'd earned in those freezing pre-dawn hours. Every sacrifice. All that accumulated wealth could be made inaccessible with one bureaucratic decision. No trial. No conviction. Just gone.

That's when it became crystal clear: the money in my bank was never really mine. It exists by the permission of others. One political decision, and a person's life savings can become inaccessible. There has to be a better option, and there is. That's why I have written this book.

What You'll Discover in These Pages

This book is everything I wish I'd known when I started. And yes, we'll be talking about crypto, but you'll learn a lot more than just that. Every expensive lesson learned. Every strategy that actually works. Every mistake you can avoid. It's your shortcut through years of trial and error.

But I need to be brutally honest: this isn't a get-rich-quick scheme. Those are scams, and you're smarter than that. This is a systematic guide to understanding and profiting from the greatest wealth transfer in human history. Some chapters will challenge everything you believe about money. Some strategies will seem too good to be true (until you verify them on chain yourself). Every principle has been battle-tested through bull markets and bear markets alike.

I've divided this book into five parts.

Part I: The Underdog's Awakening reveals why the system you trust is designed to keep you poor. You will:

- Discover how inflation is stealing 7–10% of your wealth annually while your "high-yield" savings account pays 0.5%, meaning you're guaranteed to lose purchasing power every single day.
- Learn why Bitcoin isn't just internet money but a complete parallel financial system that operates 24/7/365 without asking anyone's permission.

- Understand the Cantillon Effect and how those closest to money-printing get rich while you get poorer.
- Master asymmetric bets where you risk 1x to make 100x, the kind of opportunities that built every fortune in history but are now accessible to anyone with $100 and an internet connection.

By the end of part I, you'll never see traditional finance the same way again.

Part II: Crypto Wealth Foundations gives you a step-by-step guide that takes you from a complete beginner to a confident participant. It covers everything from opening your first exchange account (including which one and why) to buying Bitcoin at exactly the right amount: $100, enough to matter, not enough to hurt.

- Master the critical difference between CEX and DEX, where one requires permission and the other just requires your wallet.
- Learn why "not your keys, not your coins" isn't just a slogan but the difference between owning Bitcoin and owning an IOU.
- Set up hardware wallets that would take every computer on Earth longer than the universe's age to crack.
- Understand Ethereum and smart contracts without needing a computer science degree through simple analogies that make DeFi click.

No confusion, no jargon, just clear action steps you can implement today.

Part III: Market Mastery explores the psychology and cycles that separate tourists from natives. Here, you will:

- Discover the four-year Bitcoin halving cycle that's as predictable as clockwork and has never failed to produce new all-time highs.
- Learn why HODLing beats trading 95% of the time and why that 5% isn't worth the stress.
- Understand the capital rotation pattern: Bitcoin leads, Ethereum follows, large caps pump, then altseason arrives. Miss this pattern, and you'll always be two steps behind.
- Build an "untouchable portfolio" that survives 80% crashes while positioning you for massive gains.

- Master the ladder-out exit strategy that ensures you actually keep your profits instead of round-tripping from $400k back to $80k like I did.
- Learn to read market psychology so well that your own emotions become your best indicator.

Part IV: Becoming Your Own Bank reveals the DeFi strategies generating returns that traditional finance calls impossible.

- Become your own bank, earning 50%+ APY through liquidity provision while banks pay 0.05%.
- Master impermanent loss, which isn't actually a loss but the cost of earning fees that often exceed any divergence.
- Learn concentrated liquidity positions that can 10x your capital efficiency by focusing liquidity where trading actually happens.
- Discover Layer 2s where the same transaction that costs $100 on mainnet costs $0.10, making DeFi accessible to everyone, not just whales.
- Understand the velocity of money and how to make one dollar work like ten through strategic deployment across multiple protocols simultaneously.

These aren't theoretical strategies; they're generating real returns for thousands of people right now.

Part V: The Investor Mindset covers the psychological transformation that separates winners from eternal watchers.

- Find your "why" that's stronger than any 70% bear market crash. Mine evolved from escaping wage slavery to helping others do the same.
- Understand the J-curve, why everything gets worse before it gets exponentially better, and why most people quit right before the breakthrough.
- Calculate the true opportunity cost of playing it safe. That $50k sitting in savings could be $500k in ten years through DeFi.
- Master risk vs. reward mathematics that show why "risky" crypto is actually safer than "safe" fiat melting at 7% annually.

- Learn the wealth principles the rich use to get richer, from asset accumulation to compound leverage to velocity optimization. Break the poverty programming that keeps the middle class trapped in the "work, save, retire poor" cycle.

This isn't just a book full of theory from someone who only read about crypto. It's the practical playbook from someone who lost $100k in Terra Luna, round-tripped $400k to $80k, made every mistake possible, then built multi-million dollar wealth by learning what actually works. Every strategy has been tested with real money. Every principle proven. Every lesson learned the expensive way so you don't have to.

Extra Resources For You

Quick heads up: the farther into this book you get, the more technical the information becomes. DeFi protocols, liquidity provisions, and smart contract interactions can feel overwhelming on paper. That's why the team here at CryptoLabs Research created a free course along with a series of companion videos that bring these concepts to life.

Watch me actually execute these strategies on screen. See the exact buttons to click, the protocols to use, and the mistakes to avoid. Complex topics become simple when you can watch them happen in real time.

Access all the companion videos (and catch an upcoming monthly live call) free inside The DeFi University at **www.TheDeFiUniversity.com**

There, you'll find full tutorials that complement the more advanced chapters, turning theory into practical, actionable knowledge. Consider them your visual guide through the more complex sections ahead.

The Two Futures Before You

Right now, you're standing at a crossroads. Two very different futures stretch out before you. In one future, you close this book and continue as you have been. You keep trusting banks with your money. You keep losing purchasing power to inflation. You watch from the sidelines as others build wealth in crypto. Ten years from now, you look back with regret at the opportunity you missed.

In the other future, you read this book and take action. You start small, but you start today. You learn the technology. You build your portfolio systematically. You join communities of builders. You participate in the revolution. Ten years from now, you look back with gratitude at the decision that changed your family's financial trajectory forever.

The choice is yours. But understand this: not choosing is still a choice. Every day you wait is opportunity cost you'll never recover.

And yes, crypto can make you wealthy. I went from washing cars to struggling as an entrepreneur to building a multiple seven-figure net worth and total freedom to do what I want, when I want, how I want. Today, the problem isn't whether I can afford to fill up my gas tank. It's deciding which car to drive: The Lambo for speed, the Porsche for the twisties, or the '69 Dodge Charger R/T with 600+ hp for burning some rubber?

I promise I'm not trying to be douchey here, but I do want you to know what's possible. As a massive car guy who just spent a weekend replacing the transmission in my R8 (yes, I still turn my own wrenches), I genuinely love these machines. But here's what I learned after "making it": those cars won't fill the void. Neither will the houses, the travel, or the expensive meals.

I know, I know. Another rich guy telling you money won't make you happy. It's cliché because it's true. Money only solves the problems money can solve. It'll never solve the problems that truly matter. The supercar collection won't give you purpose. That new house with a view won't create meaning. The first-class flights and dinners in Miami won't provide fulfillment.

But here's what money **will** give you: **time** and **space**. Time to discover who you really are when you're not exhausted from trading your life for a paycheck. Space to solve the real problems within. Freedom to pursue what actually matters, to create something meaningful, to serve others in ways that generate genuine fulfillment.

I believe we're all here for a purpose. Whether you believe in God, the universe, or simply the beautiful randomness of existence, I think each of us has something unique we're meant to contribute to this world. A reason for being here. A gift only we can give. But as long as we stay stuck in the rat race, grinding away our best years for money that inflation destroys anyway, most people will never get the opportunity to discover what that purpose is, let alone fulfill it. **And that bothers me.**

That's why I want you to make a stupid amount of money. Not so you can buy Lambos (though enjoy them if you want; I certainly do). But so you can afford to become who you're actually meant to be. So you can break free from the cage and finally have the time, energy, and resources to pursue your life's real purpose.

The money is just the tool. *Freedom is the goal.* Purpose is the point.

More importantly, this revolution is about more than personal wealth. It's about building a financial system that's fair, transparent, and accessible to everyone. It's about removing the gatekeepers who've extracted value from working people for generations. It's about creating opportunity that's based on merit, not connections.

When you buy Bitcoin, you're not just investing; you're voting for a different future. When you use DeFi, you're not just earning yield; you're proving we don't need banks. When you build in crypto, you're not just starting a business; you're constructing tomorrow's infrastructure.

Ready to Dive In?

The traditional financial system has failed our generation. Wages that don't keep up with costs. Savings that melt from inflation. Opportunities that require connections we don't have. That system is dying, and it deserves to die. In its place, we're building something better. Something transparent. Something fair. Something that serves everyone, not just the wealthy and connected.

The question isn't whether this transformation will happen. It's already happening, and it's happening fast. The question is whether you'll be part of it. You're not too late. You're not too inexperienced. You're not too anything.

You're right on time for the greatest opportunity of our generation. Turn the page. Your education into the future of finance begins now.

Welcome to the revolution!

P.S. If you'd like to connect with me at any time and ask me questions, feel free to hop over to my Instagram @LucasRubix and shoot me a DM!

Important Disclaimers:
Please Read Before Proceeding

This book is not financial advice. The content presented here represents the author's personal experiences, opinions, and strategies in cryptocurrency markets. What worked for the author may not work for you. What failed for the author might succeed for you. Everyone's financial situation, risk tolerance, and investment goal is different.

Cryptocurrency investing carries extreme risk, including the total loss of your investment. Only invest money you can afford to lose completely without affecting your quality of life, mental health, or ability to meet financial obligations.

The regulatory landscape for cryptocurrency changes rapidly and varies by jurisdiction. What's legal today might be illegal tomorrow. What's permitted in one country might be prohibited in another. DeFi protocols, DEXs, and various cryptocurrency activities described in this book may be restricted or illegal in your location. You are responsible for understanding and complying with all applicable laws, regulations, and tax obligations in your jurisdiction.

The author is not a registered financial advisor, tax professional, or legal expert. The strategies described, including DeFi protocols, trading techniques, and tax approaches, are based on personal experience and may not be suitable or even legal for your situation. Past performance, whether the author's or that of the broader crypto market, does not guarantee future results. The cryptocurrency market is highly manipulated, largely unregulated, and subject to extreme volatility.

By reading this book, you acknowledge that you are solely responsible for your investment decisions and their consequences. Neither the author nor publisher assumes any liability for financial losses, legal issues, tax problems, or any other negative outcomes resulting from applying concepts in this book.

Mental Health and Addiction Warning

Cryptocurrency trading can become addictive and severely impact mental health. The 24/7 nature of crypto markets, extreme volatility, and potential for massive gains or losses can trigger or exacerbate mental health conditions, including anxiety, depression, mania, and addiction.

Warning signs that crypto may be negatively affecting your mental health:

- Checking prices obsessively throughout the day and night
- Losing sleep to watch charts or trade
- Feeling extreme emotional swings based on portfolio value
- Neglecting relationships, work, or responsibilities for crypto
- Investing money you need for necessities
- Feeling suicidal or severely depressed after losses
- Experiencing euphoria or mania during gains that lead to reckless decisions
- Inability to stop despite negative consequences

If you recognize these patterns, please step back and seek help. No amount of money is worth your mental health or life. Consider speaking with a mental health professional who understands behavioral addictions. Remove trading apps from your phone. Set strict boundaries around crypto engagement. Your well-being matters infinitely more than your portfolio.

If you have a history of gambling addiction, bipolar disorder, or addictive behaviors, approach cryptocurrency with extreme caution or avoid it entirely. The dynamics of crypto trading can trigger the same neural pathways as gambling. The highs are extreme, but so are the lows. Many people have lost their life savings, relationships, and mental health to crypto addiction.

Crisis Resources

If you're experiencing suicidal thoughts, contact the 988 Suicide & Crisis Lifeline (US) or your country's crisis hotline immediately.

For gambling addiction support, contact the National Council on Problem Gambling Helpline, 1-800-522-4700.

For mental health support, contact the SAMHSA National Helpline, 1-800-662-4357.

A Personal Note on Responsibility

This book shares strategies that worked during specific market conditions that may never repeat. Bitcoin's past performance from $100 to $100,000 doesn't guarantee future appreciation. The DeFi yields available at the time of writing this book may not exist by the time you read it. The regulatory environment will certainly change.

Your financial decisions are yours alone. If you choose to invest in cryptocurrency after reading this book, you must do so with full understanding of the risks. Start small. Learn continuously. Never invest more than you can afford to lose. Prioritize your mental health over potential gains.

Remember: the goal isn't to get rich at any cost. It's to build wealth sustainably while maintaining your health, relationships, and sanity. If crypto is costing you any of these, it's not worth it. No amount of money can buy back your mental health or lost relationships.

Proceed with caution, clarity, and complete personal responsibility for your choices.

If you're not comfortable with these risks and responsibilities, please close this book now. There's no shame in deciding cryptocurrency isn't for you. There are many paths to financial security that don't involve this level of risk and volatility.

Part I:

The Underdog's Awakening

1

The System Is Optional:
Why Wall Street Doesn't Want You Rich

I'm sitting in a TD Bank in downtown Vancouver, trying to wire $14,000 to buy a motorcycle I found online. It's my money. I earned it. I worked hard for it. Paid taxes on it. Have every right to do whatever I want with it. But here I am, getting interrogated like a criminal.

"What's the purpose of this transfer?" the teller asks, peering over her glasses with that particular mix of boredom and suspicion that only bank employees can master.

"Buying a motorcycle."

"From a dealership?"

"Private seller."

Her face changes. She actually leans back slightly, like I just admitted to drug trafficking. "I'll need to get my manager." Twenty minutes and a dozen questions later, they finally approve the transfer. Their generosity knows no bounds. Then they hit me with the punchline: "That'll be a $50 wire transfer fee."

Fifty dollars. For the privilege of using my own money. For the favor they're doing me by allowing me to access what's mine. I'm paying them to interrogate me about my own financial decisions.

That was the moment I knew there had to be a better way. Standing in line for 25 minutes and paying fees to access my own money after being questioned like a child, something inside me snapped.

Think about this: modern banking emerged in medieval Italy around the 14th century. In the 700 years since, humanity has invented the printing press, steam engines, electricity, automobiles, airplanes, television, computers, the internet, and smartphones. We've split the atom, decoded DNA, and put humans on the moon. We can video-chat with someone on the opposite side of the planet instantly. We've built machines that can think and cars that drive themselves.

And banks? Their biggest innovations in all that time have been the ATM in 1967 and the credit card in 1950. That's it. While we were landing on the moon, banks were figuring out how to let you access your own money without talking to a teller. While we invented the internet that connects all human knowledge instantly, banks still take three days to move money between accounts. While we were building supercomputers that fit in our pockets, banks were adding more fees and longer hold times.

Standing there in TD Bank, using essentially the same system the Medici family used 600 years ago (just with computers instead of ledgers), I kept thinking: this can't be the best humanity can do with money. I didn't have answers yet; I didn't know about Bitcoin or DeFi or any alternatives. All I knew was that in an age when smartphones packed more computing power than the rocket that took us to the moon, waiting in line to beg permission to use my own money was insane.

The Architecture of Control

The traditional financial system isn't designed to serve you. It's designed to control you. Every aspect, every friction point, every fee is intentional. They need you to believe managing money is too complex for regular people like you and me. They need you to be dependent on their infrastructure. They need you to ask permission for everything.

Think about how absurd this actually is. You work forty hours a week, or, in my case, twelve-hour days on the rigs. Your employer direct-deposits your paycheck into your bank account. That money is supposedly yours. But try to use it freely and watch what happens.

Want to withdraw $5,000 cash? They may or may not be able to do it that, and if they can, they'll need to know why. Want to send it internationally? Three to five business days and documentation required. Want to buy something from a private seller? Prepare for the inquisition. Want to access it on a Sunday? Sorry, banks are closed and your money is temporarily unavailable.

We've normalized this insanity. We accept that our money has business hours. We accept that transfers take days in an era where I can stream 4K video instantly to my phone. We accept that we need permission to use what we earned with our own bodies and time.

But here's what really burns me: while they're controlling our access to our money, while they're charging us fees for the privilege of using it, they're using that same money to make themselves rich. That's the real scam nobody talks about.

How Banks Actually Make Money (Spoiler: It's Your Money)

When I was on the rigs, I thought banks were these sophisticated institutions doing complex financial wizardry to earn their profits. Then I learned their business model, and I almost laughed at how simple the scam is.

You deposit $10,000. The bank immediately lends out $9,000 of it through fractional reserve banking. They charge the borrower 10% interest while paying you 0.05%. Let's look at those real numbers, because they matter. Your $10,000 at 0.05% annual interest earns you $5 per year. Five dollars. That's forty-two cents per month. You could find more money in your couch cushions.

Meanwhile, that $9,000 they lent out at 10% generates $1,000 per year for them. They're making 200 times more on your money than you are. And that's just the first iteration. Here's where it gets really crazy. That $9,000 they lent out? It gets deposited in another account. That bank lends out $8,100. Which gets deposited and lent out again. And again. And again. Through this process, your original $10,000 becomes $100,000 in the system. All of it earning interest for banks. All of it created from nothing.

This is fractional reserve banking. It's literally creating money from thin air, and it's perfectly legal. The banks get rich. The borrowers pay interest on money that didn't exist until they borrowed it. And you? You get your forty-two cents per month, pay a $50 wire fee when you want to use your money, and endure lectures about how they're protecting you.

I remember getting my first "interest payment" after keeping $20,000 in savings for a full year. Eight dollars and thirty-three cents. I spent more on parking to go to the bank than I earned in interest. Meanwhile, the bank made thousands lending my money to others. That's when I understood: savings accounts aren't for saving. They're for banks to access cheap capital.

The Cantillon Effect: Why You're Always Last in Line

Richard Cantillon figured this out in the 1700s, but it's more relevant today than ever. When new money enters the economy, it doesn't affect everyone equally. The people who get it first can spend it before prices adjust. The people who get it last receive it after inflation has already occurred.

For example: In 2020 and 2021, the Federal Reserve printed over $6 trillion. That's $6,000,000,000,000 created from nothing. Where did it go?

First, to banks at near-zero interest rates. They used it to buy assets and make loans. Then to corporations, who borrowed cheap money for stock buybacks. Then to asset holders, who watched their stocks and real estate explode in value. By the time that money reached regular workers through wages or stimulus checks, what had happened?

Lumber was up 400%. My buddy trying to build a house watched his dream evaporate as materials became unaffordable. House prices up 30% or more. Food up 20%. Families choosing between groceries and gas. Everything you need to live became more expensive because the money had already flowed through the system, pushing up prices along the way.

It's not by accident, either. Those closest to the money printer get wealthy. Everyone else gets inflation. Every round of money printing is a wealth transfer from people who work for money to people who own assets. And they've been running this play for decades.

The Money Printer Goes Brrr

Remember March 2020? The world shut down, markets crashed, and the Federal Reserve fired up the money printer like never before. Jerome Powell literally said they had "unlimited" ammunition. Unlimited. As in no limit to how much money they could create.

They created more money in 18 months than existed in the first 200 years of American history. Not earned through productivity. Not backed by gold or silver or anything real. Just typed into existence on computers.

The memes about the money printer going "brrr" were funny, but the reality is devastating. Every dollar created makes existing dollars worth less. It's a hidden tax on anyone holding cash or earning wages. But here's the sick part: they knew exactly what they were doing.

While telling us inflation was "transitory," they were printing trillions. While working people wondered why groceries suddenly cost double, they were bailing out corporations. While young people got priced out of ever owning homes, they were ensuring asset prices went to the moon.

I watched this happen to a lot of people I knew who prioritized "saving" over investing in assets. Guys who'd saved for years to buy houses suddenly couldn't afford them. Families who'd been responsible, who'd done everything right, watched their savings become worthless. The government and the Federal Reserve stole from an entire generation through money printing, and they did it in broad daylight.

The Hidden Tax of Inflation

Inflation isn't some natural phenomenon like weather. It's a policy choice. It's a hidden tax that transfers wealth from savers to debtors, from workers to asset owners, from you to them. The government tells you inflation is 2% to 3%. That's a lie so bold it's insulting. Ask anyone who actually buys groceries, pays rent, or fills up their gas tank. Real inflation, the kind working people experience, is closer to 10% to 15% annually.

Let me show you what this means with real numbers.

Say you've saved $50,000. You worked years for that money. Sacrificed. Skipped vacations. Drove old cars. You did everything right. At 10% real inflation, that $50,000 loses $5,000 in purchasing power every year. In a decade, your $50,000 buys what $25,000 buys today.

You're not just failing to grow wealth. You're actively becoming poorer by being responsible and saving money. The system punishes savers and rewards debtors. And who's the biggest debtor? The government, with $33 trillion in debt that gets easier to pay back as they inflate the currency.

This is why our parents could buy a house on one income, but now most people can't afford a house even on two incomes. This is why our grandparents could pay for college with summer jobs but most people now will have student loans until they're fifty. The money is broken, and it's broken on purpose.

Why Saving Guarantees Poverty

Every financial advisor tells you to save. Have an emergency fund. Be responsible. Live below your means. It's good advice in principle, but it's a guaranteed path to poverty in practice.

Let's say you're disciplined. You save $1,000 per month in a savings account paying 0.5% interest. After 30 years, you'll have $360,000 nominally. Sounds good, right? Now adjust for 7% inflation (which is conservative). That $360,000 has the purchasing power of about $47,000 in today's money.

You saved for thirty years to end up with less purchasing power than one year of your current salary. That's not building wealth. That's running in place while the treadmill speeds up.

Meanwhile, the person who borrowed $360,000 thirty years ago for real estate? They paid it back with inflated dollars worth a fraction of what they borrowed. The house appreciated while the debt got inflated away. They got rich using the bank's money while most people got poorer saving money.

This isn't an accident. The system is designed to force you into debt and speculation. Save money? You're guaranteed to lose purchasing power. Invest in stocks? Maybe you'll keep up with inflation if you're lucky. Borrow money to buy assets? Now you're playing the game they want you to play, taking risks you shouldn't have to take.

You Can Opt Out If You Want To

But here's what they don't want you to know: their entire system is optional. Every rule, every restriction, every permission requirement exists only if you choose to play their game. There's another system being built right now that operates on completely different principles. Bitcoin!

Bitcoin doesn't ask permission. It doesn't have business hours. It doesn't charge you $50 to use your own money. It doesn't require interrogation to make transfers. It just works, 24/7/365, for anyone with an internet connection.

When I finally bought Bitcoin (after that motorcycle purchase opened my eyes to how broken traditional banking is), the difference was shocking. I could send $10,000 across the world in minutes for a few dollars in fees. No questions. No managers. No permission slips. Just me controlling my money directly.

DeFi takes it even further (and we'll be talking a lot about it in later chapters of this book). Instead of begging banks for loans, you can borrow instantly against collateral. Instead of accepting 0.05% interest, you can earn 5% to 10% by lending directly to others. Instead of paying banks to be the middlemen, you become the bank and earn the fees yourself.

This isn't some theoretical future. Millions of people are using this parallel system right now. They're sending money without permission. They're earning yield without banks. They're building wealth without playing by rules designed to keep them poor.

The system that interrogated me about buying a motorcycle, that charged me $50 for accessing my own money, that pays me nothing while using my deposits to get rich? That system is optional. You can opt out today. The permission architecture has power only if you submit to it. The moment you hold your own Bitcoin, you're no longer asking permission. The moment you use DeFi, you're no longer begging for access. The moment you understand that their entire system is optional, you're free.

They tried to fight crypto, and they failed spectacularly. China banned Bitcoin mining in 2021, and the network recovered in months. India tried banning crypto trading, and their Supreme Court overturned it. The SEC sued everyone they could, but Bitcoin ETFs got approved anyway. Every attack, every ban, every attempt to kill it only proved why we need it more.

The harder they fought, the stronger crypto became. Why? Because people fundamentally want to be free. We don't like being controlled. We don't like asking permission to use what's ours. We don't like arbitrary rules designed to keep us dependent. Every regulatory crackdown just reminded more people why a permissionless system matters.

They spread fear about crypto being used by criminals, while banks laundered trillions for cartels. They called it a bubble, while printing trillions from nothing. They said it would fail, while it grew from zero to $3 trillion. They tried to regulate it into looking like the traditional system, not understanding that making crypto like traditional finance defeats the entire purpose.

But here's what they never understood: you can't uninvent an idea whose time has come. You can't put the genie back in the bottle. You can't make people forget that an alternative exists. Their entire scam collapses the moment enough people realize the cage door is open.

The financial revolution isn't coming. It's here. Despite all the efforts to stop it, millions of people are already using a parallel financial system that doesn't require their permission. The only question is whether you'll walk through that open door or stay in the cage, paying $50 fees to access your own money while they get rich using it.

I walked through that door. Millions of others have, too. Here, your money is actually yours. The system is optional. You just need someone to show you the exit.

2

Bitcoin 101:
The Foundation of a New Financial World

My dad came to Canada with nothing. No money. No connections. Didn't speak English. An immigrant who believed in the promise that hard work equals success. And he worked. Believe me, he worked. Double shifts. Weekend jobs. Eighteen-hour days. Whatever it took to provide for his family.

He taught me that hard work was the answer to everything. Wake up early. Stay late. Never complain. Keep grinding. For his generation, maybe that was enough. You could work hard, save money, buy a house, retire with dignity.

But he taught me only half the equation. Hard work gets you to the starting line. But in a system where money loses value every year, where wages never keep pace with asset prices, where the rules change based on who's in power, hard work alone just makes you tired.

The other half of the equation? Understanding money itself. How it works. Who controls it. Why it loses value. And, most importantly, how to store your hard work in something that can't be stolen through inflation or frozen by decree.

That's what Bitcoin taught me. Not just to work hard, but to work smart. To store the value of my labor in something that appreciates rather than depreciates. To own something that actually belongs to me.

A Brief History of Money (And Why It All Led to Bitcoin)

To understand why Bitcoin matters, you need to understand how we got to this broken system.

Money started as barter. I'll trade you three chickens for your goat. But barter has obvious problems. What if you don't want chickens? What if your goat is worth 3.5 chickens? How do you make change?

So humans developed commodity money: shells, beads, stones, anything scarce and hard to forge. Eventually, we settled on precious metals. Gold and silver had perfect monetary properties: scarce, divisible, durable, recognizable, portable (to a degree).

For thousands of years, gold was money. It couldn't be created from nothing. Governments couldn't print it. Its supply grew slowly and predictably, about 2% annually from mining. But gold had problems, too. It was heavy. It was also hard to divide for small transactions, expensive to transport and store, and difficult to check for purity.

So we created paper certificates backed by gold. "I promise to pay the bearer one ounce of gold." These IOUs were more convenient than carrying gold. Then came the trick. Bankers realized they could issue more certificates than they had gold. After all, not everyone would redeem at once, right? This was the birth of fractional reserve banking, the first major departure from sound money.

In 1913, the Federal Reserve was created, centralizing control of US money. In 1933, Roosevelt confiscated private gold ownership. Think about that. The government literally made it illegal to own gold and forced citizens to sell it to them at a fixed price. At the Bretton Woods conference in 1944, delegates from 44 nations made the U.S. dollar the world's reserve currency, still backed by gold.

Then in 1971, Nixon ended gold convertibility entirely. He called it a "temporary" measure. Fifty-three years later, it's still temporary. Put simply, we all got rug-pulled.

Since 1971, we've had pure fiat currency: money backed by nothing but government promises. And what happened? The U.S. dollar has lost 96% of its purchasing power. Wealth inequality has exploded. Boom and bust cycles have intensified. The money printer has become the solution to every problem.

This is the system Bitcoin was designed to replace.

Understanding the Bitcoin White Paper

On October 31, 2008, while the global financial system was melting down, someone using the name Satoshi Nakamoto published a nine-page document that would change everything: "Bitcoin: A Peer-to-Peer Electronic Cash System."

Let me break down what this revolutionary document actually says, because understanding it changes how you see money forever. The core problem Satoshi identified was simple but profound: electronic payments require trusting financial institutions. These institutions can reverse transactions, freeze accounts, charge high fees, and exclude people. They're central points of failure. When they fail, everyone suffers.

The solution Satoshi proposed was elegant: a peer-to-peer network where transactions are verified by cryptographic proof instead of trust. No middlemen needed. No permission required. No single point of failure.

Here's how it actually works. When you send Bitcoin, you digitally sign the transaction with your private key. This proves you own the Bitcoin and authorized the transfer. Your signature is mathematically impossible to forge, which is the kind of certainty that human institutions can never provide.

All transactions are recorded in a public ledger called the blockchain. Think of it as a book where every page contains a list of transactions, and each new page references the previous one, creating an unbreakable chain stretching back to the very first Bitcoin transaction.

To add a new page to this book, computers around the world compete to solve complex mathematical puzzles. This process, called proof of work, requires real-world energy and makes it extremely expensive to attack the network. The first to solve the puzzle gets rewarded with new Bitcoin. This brilliant design aligns incentives: those securing the network profit from its success.

The consensus mechanism is perhaps the most revolutionary part. Everyone has a copy of the entire transaction history. The longest chain, the one with the most computational work, is accepted as truth. To change history, you'd need to redo all that work, which becomes exponentially harder as time passes. After just six confirmations, a Bitcoin transaction is essentially irreversible.

And then there's the monetary policy, coded in stone: only 21 million Bitcoin will ever exist. I'm going to repeat that. There will only ever be 21 million Bitcoin. The rate of new Bitcoin creation halves every four years until it stops entirely around 2140. This predictable, unchangeable monetary policy is revolutionary. For the first time in history, we have money with a supply that can't be manipulated by any government, corporation, or individual.

How Bitcoin Solves Every Problem Fiat Created

Let's map out exactly how Bitcoin addresses each failure of government money. The problem of infinite money printing has plagued every fiat currency in history. Governments always promise restraint, but when crisis hits, the printers turn on. The Federal Reserve created more dollars in 2020 than in the first two centuries of American history. Bitcoin's solution is elegant: 21 million coins maximum, enforced by code, not promises. No emergency, no war, no pandemic can change this.

Centralized control means your money exists at the whim of whoever's in power. One day you're allowed to buy what you want; the next day certain purchases are forbidden. One day your account works; the next it's frozen. We've seen this play out repeatedly, from Cyprus bail-ins to Canadian account freezes. Bitcoin operates on a decentralized network with no single point of control. No CEO to bribe. No server to shut down. No headquarters to raid.

Currency debasement is the silent thief. Governments set "inflation targets" of 2% as if slowly robbing you is acceptable. But real inflation runs much higher. Bitcoin's supply inflation decreases every four years and eventually reaches zero. It's designed to increase in purchasing power over time, not decrease.

The lack of transparency in traditional finance is staggering. Federal Reserve meetings happen behind closed doors. Banks use your deposits for undisclosed investments. With Bitcoin, every transaction is visible on the blockchain. The supply is known to the exact satoshi. The code is open-source. Transparency isn't a feature; it's the foundation.

Geographic restrictions trap billions of dollars in failing economies. Capital controls prevent people from escaping collapsing currencies. Banking hours mean your money sleeps while you might need it. Bitcoin operates 24/7/365 globally with 10-minute settlement anywhere on Earth. It doesn't recognize borders because math doesn't have a passport.

The Properties That Make Bitcoin Superior Money

Bitcoin has achieved something remarkable: it's better money than anything humans have used before. Let's examine why.

Perfect scarcity. Gold is scarce, but we don't know exactly how much exists underground or in asteroids. Bitcoin, on the other hand, offers mathematical certainty: exactly 21 million coins, forever. This absolute scarcity has never existed in any form of money throughout history.

Infinite divisibility. Gold is hard to divide for small transactions. Dollars only divide into pennies, whereas Bitcoin divides into 100 million satoshis per coin, allowing you to send as little as 0.00000001 Bitcoin (roughly $0.001 today). Even if each Bitcoin becomes worth millions, it can still function as everyday currency.

Weightless portability. A million dollars in gold weighs 35 pounds. Cash is bulky and suspicious in large amounts. Wire transfers are slow, expensive, and surveilled. But Bitcoin? It moves at internet speed across any border, weightless and unstoppable. You can carry a billion dollars in your head by memorizing twelve words.

Instant verification. Gold requires expertise to verify its purity. Cash has sophisticated counterfeits. Bank dollars are just database entries you must trust. Bitcoin can be verified instantly by anyone running a node. Every transaction traces back to its origin, proving authenticity through mathematics, not trust.

Permanent durability. Gold doesn't corrode, but it can be physically stolen. Cash degrades and burns. Banks fail and take deposits with them. Bitcoin, however, exists as information across thousands of computers globally. As long as even one copy of the blockchain survives anywhere in the world, Bitcoin survives.

The Network Effect That Makes Bitcoin Unstoppable

Bitcoin isn't just superior technology; it has an insurmountable head start that grows stronger daily through multiple reinforcing network effects.

First, the security network dwarfs all competition. Bitcoin commands more computing power than all other cryptocurrencies combined, and this protective moat expands every day. The cost to attack Bitcoin now rivals the resources of a major nation-state, and even then, success isn't guaranteed. This makes Bitcoin the most secure computer network humanity has ever created.

Second, deep liquidity creates real utility. Bitcoin trades on every exchange globally with such depth that you can buy or sell millions without significantly moving the price. This liquidity transforms Bitcoin from a speculative asset into functional money. No other cryptocurrency comes close to matching this market depth.

Third, thousands of brilliant developers continuously improve the protocol, working not for a company but for the idea itself. This decentralized development ensures Bitcoin evolves through consensus rather than corporate decree, making it truly antifragile and adaptive.

Fourth, the surrounding infrastructure took fifteen years to build and would take decades to replicate. Bitcoin ATMs dot the globe, payment processors integrate it everywhere, custody solutions protect institutional holdings, and hardware wallets secure individual wealth. Any competitor faces the daunting task of rebuilding this entire ecosystem from scratch.

Finally, perhaps most powerful is the belief network. Millions of holders see themselves not as investors but as revolutionaries building a new monetary system. This ideological commitment creates diamond hands that hold regardless of price, providing stability that pure speculation never could. You can't manufacture this kind of conviction.

The Lindy Effect suggests that the longer something survives, the longer it's likely to continue surviving. Bitcoin has weathered fifteen years of attacks, bans, crashes, forks, and countless obituaries declaring its death. Every crisis that fails to kill it proves its antifragility and extends its probable lifespan. Time itself has become Bitcoin's ally.

Common Bitcoin Criticisms Debunked

"Bitcoin is too volatile." Yes, short-term. But zoom out to any four-year period and it's always higher. Volatility is the price of adoption. As Bitcoin grows from $2 trillion to $10 trillion to eventually $100 trillion market cap, its volatility naturally decreases.

"Bitcoin wastes energy." Bitcoin uses energy to secure the network. That's not waste; it's the cost of incorruptible money. Moreover, Bitcoin mining incentivizes renewable energy by monetizing stranded energy. The global banking system uses 56 times more energy than Bitcoin.

"Bitcoin is too slow." Bitcoin settles in 10 minutes globally with irreversible finality. Try sending a wire on Sunday. For instant payments, Lightning Network enables millisecond transactions for fractions of a penny.

"Governments will ban it." They've tried. China banned mining; hash rate recovered in months. India tried banning; supreme court overruled. Banning Bitcoin is like banning math.

"It's used by criminals." Less than 1% of Bitcoin transactions are illicit versus 2–5% of fiat transactions. The transparent blockchain makes Bitcoin terrible for crime. The dollar remains criminals' preferred currency.

Your Journey Begins with Nine Pages

Ready for some homework? Read the Bitcoin white paper. Nine pages that changed the world. Go to bitcoin.org and find it.

It'll be confusing at first. Technical concepts will fly over your head. You might understand 10% on your first read. Read it anyway. This is your initiation into a new way of thinking about money. Even if 90% goes over your head, that 10% you grasp will be revolutionary. Read it once now. Again in a few weeks. Again in half a year. Each time, you'll understand more. Each reading deepens your conviction.

Bitcoin is hope encoded in mathematics. Hope for everyone excluded from traditional finance. For immigrants sending money home without Western Union's extortion. For activists whose bank accounts get frozen. For savers watching their purchasing power evaporate. For anyone who believes money should serve people, not governments.

Every Bitcoin you own is a vote against the fiat system. It's opting out of guaranteed debasement. It's choosing mathematics over politics, code over corruption, transparency over backroom deals. The revolution started with those nine pages in 2008. It continues with every person who chooses freedom over permission. The question isn't whether Bitcoin will succeed. The math guarantees that. The question is whether you'll participate in its success.

3

The Fiat Trap:
How Inflation and Banks Steal Your Wealth

There's a theft happening right now, in your wallet, in your bank account, in your paycheck. It's not dramatic. No one's breaking down your door. No sirens are going off. It's happening so slowly, so quietly, that most people never notice until it's too late.

The thief is inflation, and the weapon is fiat currency: money backed by nothing but government promises and printed at will.

Let me show you the scale of this theft. Then I'll show you the escape route.

The Worst Trade You Make Every Day

Here's the insanity nobody talks about: most people wake up at 5 a.m., commute in traffic, work for 8 to 10 hours, deal with bosses they don't like and deadlines that stress them out, all to earn money that's guaranteed to lose value. They're literally trading their finite life hours for something programmed to become worthless.

Think about that trade. Your time, energy, youth, health, moments with family, all exchanged for paper that loses 7–10% of its value annually. You're working harder than ever to earn money that's worth less than ever. It's the worst trade in human history, and billions of people make it every single day.

Note that I'm not slamming work. Personally, I love working hard. It gives me a sense of fulfillment. Of direction. Of contribution. Of purpose. But, if I'm going to trade my precious time for money (and we all do), I want to capture that energy into something that will not only preserve my efforts but multiply them.

Remember those years I spent on the oil rigs? I was away from home for weeks at a time, enduring −40° weather, destroying my body, all for dollars that have already lost 40% or more of their value since then. I traded irreplaceable time and health for replaceable, depreciating paper. If that's not insanity, what is? Even worse, I didn't know about crypto back then, so I invested those dollars in mutual funds that not only failed to keep up with inflation but also had fees that ate away any meaningful growth.

Your parents worked the same jobs for fewer nominal dollars that could buy more. A factory worker in 1970 could support a family, buy a house, send kids to college. Today? That same job, adjusted for inflation, barely covers rent. Not because the work became less valuable, but because the money became less valuable.

Every Fiat Currency Goes to Zero

Every fiat currency in history has gone to zero. Every single one. The Roman denarius, the Chinese flying money, the French assignat, the German papiermark, the Zimbabwean dollar, the Venezuelan bolivar. Thousands of currencies, all following the same pattern: creation, debasement, hyperinflation, death.

One study found the average lifespan of a fiat currency is **just 27 years**. The U.S. dollar has outlasted that average because of its global reserve status, but it's following the same trajectory, just in slow motion. Since 1971, when Nixon "temporarily" suspended gold convertibility, the dollar has lost **over 96% of its purchasing power.**

The Roman Empire showed us exactly how this ends. They started with the silver denarius, nearly pure silver. Strong money for a strong empire. But wars cost money. Bread and circuses cost money. Maintaining an empire costs money.

Instead of living within their means, they did what every government does: they debased the currency. Over 200 years, they gradually reduced the silver content from 95% to less than 2%. Citizens weren't told their money was becoming worthless. They just noticed that prices kept rising, that their savings bought less each year, that working harder somehow made them poorer.

By the end, Roman soldiers refused payment in denarii. They wanted payment in goods, land, anything but the worthless coins. The empire that conquered the world was brought down by bad money.

We're doing the exact same thing today, just digitally. Instead of diluting silver content, we dilute dollar supply. Instead of shaving coins, we create digits in computers. The mechanism is different, but the pattern is identical.

Nixon's 1971 Rug Pull

August 15, 1971. President Nixon appears on television and announces he's "temporarily" suspending the convertibility of dollars to gold. Temporary. That was 53 years ago.

Before that date, foreign governments could exchange $35 for an ounce of gold. This limited how many dollars could exist. There had to be some relationship between paper and reality. After that date, dollars became backed by nothing except government promises.

What happened next was predictable. The money supply exploded. In 1971, there was about $650 billion in circulation. Today, there's over $21 trillion. That's a 32-fold increase. Did the economy grow 3,200%? Did productivity increase 3,200%? Did we create 32 times more value? No. We just created 32 times more paper claims on the same pie.

Here's How Money Printing Actually Works

When the Federal Reserve wants to create money, they don't even need paper. They log into a computer, type numbers into their account, and voilà—billions more dollars exist. They use these newly created dollars to buy government bonds from banks. The banks now have cash they need to lend out to earn interest. More loans mean more money in circulation. More money chasing the same goods means higher prices.

But here's the truly evil part: this new money doesn't distribute evenly. It flows first to banks, then to corporations, then to asset holders, and finally, maybe, eventually to workers through wages. By the time it reaches regular people, prices have already adjusted upward.

I watched this play out in real time during 2020–2021. The Fed created $6 trillion from nothing. Banker were buying second homes. Corporate executives were getting record bonuses. Meanwhile, the guys and gals who actually got their hands dirty for work were wondering why groceries suddenly cost double.

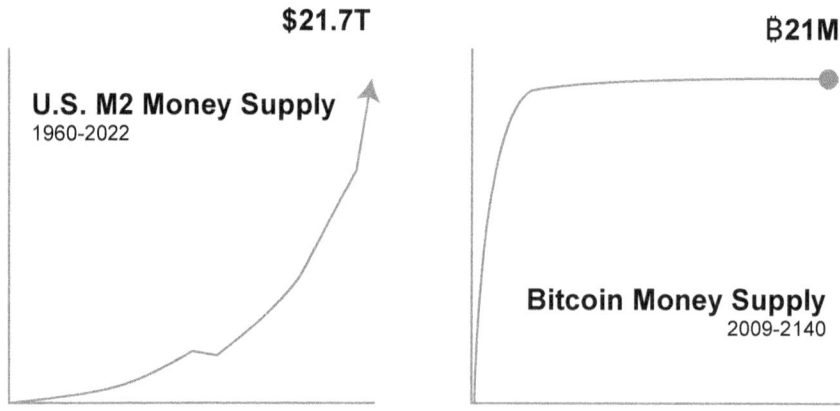

The Debt Trap and Your Melting Savings

The fiat system requires ever-increasing debt to function. This isn't a flaw; it's the core mechanism. When money is created by lending, total debt must continuously expand or the system collapses. Think about this insanity: every dollar in existence was borrowed into existence. Someone, somewhere, owes that dollar plus interest. But if all money is borrowed, where does the money to pay interest come from? More borrowing. It's a mathematical impossibility. The system requires infinite growth on a finite planet.

This is why lenders make debt so attractive. Zero percent financing. Buy now, pay later. Student loans for everyone. Credit cards with rewards. They need you in debt because your debt is what creates their money. The average American will pay over $300,000 in interest over their lifetime. Three hundred thousand dollars transferred from their labor to banks for the privilege of using money the banks created from nothing. You work for it. They type it into existence. And somehow you owe them interest on it.

Meanwhile, if you try to be "responsible" and save instead of borrowing, you get punished even worse. When I first started saving money from the rigs, I was super proud of myself. Finally building something. Finally being responsible. I had $50,000 saved up, sitting in a "high-yield" savings account paying 0.5%.

That $50,000 was earning me $250 per year. Meanwhile, inflation was running at minimum 7%, meaning I was losing $3,500 in purchasing power annually. My reward for being responsible was a guaranteed loss of $3,250 per year. I was literally paying the bank $3,250 annually to hold my money while they lent it out at 10% or more.

Whether you borrow or save, the house wins. Borrow, and you pay them interest on money they created from nothing. Save, and you lose purchasing power while they profit from lending your money to others. This is the trap most people never escape. They work, they save, they do everything "right," and they get poorer every year. Not because they're lazy or stupid, but because the game is rigged against anyone trying to build wealth through traditional means.

The One-Dollar Experiment

Let me show you something that changed how I see money forever. Take one dollar from ten years ago and see what happened to it in two different scenarios.

Scenario one: You save it responsibly in a bank account. Today, you still have one dollar. Except that dollar lost 40% of its purchasing power to inflation. Your dollar buys what 60 cents bought ten years ago. You did everything right and lost 40%.

Scenario two: You convert that dollar to Bitcoin when it was around $500. That dollar bought you 0.002 Bitcoin. Today, with Bitcoin around $100,000, that 0.002 Bitcoin is worth $200.

One dollar saved traditionally: 40% loss. One dollar converted to Bitcoin: 20,000% gain.

That's not investment advice. That's math. One system is designed to lose value. The other is designed to gain value. Every dollar you held in fiat instead of Bitcoin cost you $199 in opportunity.

This is where Bitcoin becomes not just an investment but a lifeboat from a sinking ship. Bitcoin's fixed supply of 21 million coins can't be changed by any government, crisis, or vote. It's monetary policy written in code, not subject to human weakness.

But Bitcoin was just the beginning. It proved we can create money without governments. Then Ethereum proved we can create financial services without banks. DeFi built an entire parallel economy where you can lend, borrow, trade, and invest without any traditional institutions.

While your bank pays you 0.5% on savings, DeFi protocols pay 5–10% for the same service. While banks take three days for transfers, crypto moves in minutes globally. While getting a loan requires months of paperwork and begging, DeFi lets you borrow instantly against collateral.

The entire corrupt system that's been stealing from you through inflation, fees, and restrictions? It's now optional. There's a complete alternative financial system operating right now. Millions of people are already using it. They're earning real yields instead of watching their savings melt. They're building wealth in assets that appreciate instead of currencies that depreciate.

Now You're In Control of Your Money

For the first time in history, we have an alternative. Previous generations suffering currency debasement had nowhere to run. When the Roman denarius collapsed, there was no opting out. When the Weimar mark hyperinflated, Germans couldn't escape. When the Venezuelan bolivar became worthless, citizens were trapped.

Now we have Bitcoin, Ethereum, and thousands of digital assets that can't be printed, can't be debased, can't be confiscated without your key. We have DeFi protocols that provide every banking service without the bank. We have a complete parallel economy that operates on code instead of corruption.

This changes everything. Governments can't rob their citizens through inflation if citizens can exit to crypto. Central banks can't fund endless wars if people stop accepting their paper. The entire fiat scam works only if we have no alternative.

Now we do.

Every day you hold fiat is a day you're volunteering to be robbed. Every paycheck you don't convert is value you'll never recover. This isn't about getting rich quick. It's about not getting poor slowly.

The solution is simple but requires courage most people don't have. Start converting fiat to crypto. Not all at once; you still need fiat for daily expenses. But systematically, consistently, purposefully.

Every paycheck, convert some to Bitcoin or Ethereum. Build positions in the only monetary systems that can't be debased. Use DeFi to earn real yields on stablecoins instead of watching savings accounts melt. This book will definitely help you create a game plan.

The Choice Before You

Right now, you face a simple choice with profound consequences.

Option 1: Keep your wealth in fiat. Accept the 7–10% annual loss to inflation. Hope your wages keep up (they won't). Trust that governments will stop printing (they can't). Watch your purchasing power evaporate year after year.

Option 2: Convert devaluing fiat to appreciating crypto assets. Bitcoin for pristine collateral. Ethereum for DeFi access. Stablecoins earning real yields instead of melting in banks. Build wealth in the new system while escaping the old.

The fiat trap has been set for generations. But now, finally, we have the key to escape. Bitcoin opened the door. Ethereum built the bridge. DeFi created the destination. The Roman Empire fell because they debased their currency until it was worthless. Every empire in history has fallen the same way. The American empire is following the same pattern.

But you don't have to fall with it. For the first time in history, you can opt out. You can exit the burning building. You can participate in the new financial system being built on mathematics instead of politics.

The greatest theft in human history is happening right now in your wallet. But the greatest opportunity in human history is happening in crypto, DeFi, and the parallel economy Bitcoin started.

Which side of history will you be on?

4

Blockchain Demystified:
The Hidden Tech Changing Everything

When I first heard about blockchain, I thought it was some complex computer science thing that only programmers could understand. Smart contracts sounded like legal documents written by robots. DeFi seemed like another Wall Street scheme with extra steps.

I was completely wrong. These technologies are actually simple concepts wrapped in technical jargon. Once you understand the basics, you'll see they're not complicated at all. They're elegant solutions to ancient problems.

More importantly, understanding this foundation is crucial for everything we'll build on later. In part III, I'll show you how to read market cycles and build wealth systematically. In part IV, we'll dive deep into DeFi strategies that generate 30–50% or higher returns. But none of that works if you don't understand what you're actually buying and using.

So let's demystify this revolution. By the end of this chapter, you'll understand blockchain better than 99% of people, including many who already own crypto.

Blockchain: The Ledger Everyone Can Read But No One Can Forge

Forget everything you've heard about blockchain being complex. At its core, the blockchain is just a notebook that everyone has a copy of.

Imagine we're in a small village, and we need to track who owes what to whom. We could have one person keep the records, but what if they lie? What if they lose the notebook? What if they charge fees for every entry?

Instead, we give everyone in the village an identical notebook. When someone makes a transaction, they announce it to everyone. Everyone writes it down in their notebook. Now, if someone tries to cheat by changing an old entry, their notebook won't match everyone else's. The cheater is immediately obvious.

That's blockchain: a shared ledger that everyone can read, everyone has a copy of, and no one can forge because any changes would be obvious to everyone else.

But here's where it gets brilliant. In our village example, people could still disagree about which transactions to write down. So blockchain adds a mechanism: every ten minutes (for Bitcoin), all the new transactions get bundled into a "block." To add this block to the chain, computers compete to solve a complex math puzzle. The winner gets rewarded with new Bitcoin.

This is genius for three reasons. First, it takes real energy and money to solve these puzzles, so attackers can't just spam fake transactions. Second, each block references the previous one, creating a chain going back to the very first transaction. To change history, you'd need to redo all that computational work. Third, the longest chain wins, so attackers would need to out-compute the entire honest network.

The result? A ledger that doesn't need a bank to maintain it, a government to enforce it, or any trusted third party to verify it. Just math and consensus.

The Double-Spend Problem Finally Solved

Before Bitcoin, digital money had a fatal flaw. Digital files can be copied infinitely. If I send you a photo, I still have the photo. So if I send you digital money, how do you know I haven't sent the same money to someone else? This is called the double-spend problem, and it's why we used to need banks for digital transactions. Banks were the trusted third party tracking who had what.

Bitcoin solved this without banks. When you send Bitcoin, you're not sending a file. You're broadcasting a message to the entire network that says, "I'm transferring ownership of these specific coins to this specific address." The network validates your ownership of those coins and records the transfer, and now everyone knows those coins belong to the recipient.

Try to spend them again? The network rejects it because everyone's ledger shows you already spent them. No bank needed. No trust required. Just mathematical proof witnessed by thousands of computers globally.

The profundity of this breakthrough can't be overstated. For the first time in history, we can transfer value digitally without trusting anyone. That's the foundation everything else builds on.

Smart Contracts: If–Then Statements That Run Forever

If blockchain lets us transfer value without banks, smart contracts let us create agreements without lawyers. But don't let the name fool you. Smart contracts aren't smart, and they're not really contracts in the legal sense. They're just programs that run exactly as coded, forever, without possibility of change.

Think of them as cosmic vending machines. You insert the required inputs (money, data, whatever the contract specifies), and you automatically get the programmed outputs. No negotiation. No interpretation. No possibility of breach. The code is the contract.

Here's a simple example. You want to bet me $100 that Bitcoin will hit $150,000 by December 31st. Traditionally, we'd need a bookie to hold the money and pay the winner. But bookies can run off with the money or refuse to pay.

With a smart contract, we both send $100 to the contract. On December 31st, the contract checks Bitcoin's price from multiple sources (called oracles). If it's above $150,000, the contract automatically sends you $200. If not, I get the $200. No trust required. No possibility of non-payment. Just code executing exactly as programmed.

Now scale this concept. Insurance automatically pays valid claims. Loans automatically liquidate if collateral drops too low. Supply chains automatically release payment when goods arrive. Every agreement that currently requires trust and enforcement can become trustless code.

This is what Ethereum enabled. While Bitcoin is programmable money, Ethereum is a programmable economy. Smart contracts are the building blocks of an entirely new financial system, which brings us to...

DeFi: The New Financial System

DeFi (decentralized finance) is what happens when you rebuild every financial service using smart contracts. No banks. No brokers. No middlemen. Just code providing financial services to anyone with internet.

Let me make this concrete. When you deposit money in a bank, they pay you 0.05% and lend it out at 15%. The bank pockets the 14.95% difference. With DeFi lending protocols like Aave or Compound, there is no bank. Lenders earn 5–10% directly from borrowers who pay 7–12%. The smart contract just matches lenders with borrowers and enforces the terms. No buildings, employees, or executives needed.

When you trade stocks, market makers profit from the spread between buy and sell prices. With DeFi exchanges like Uniswap, there are no market makers. Liquidity providers deposit assets into pools. Traders swap against these pools. The protocol automatically adjusts prices based on supply and demand. Liquidity providers earn fees from every trade.

We'll dive deep into specific DeFi strategies in part IV, including how to earn 30–50%+ APY through liquidity provision and yield farming. But for now, understand this: DeFi isn't improving traditional finance. It's replacing it entirely with something fundamentally different.

Traditional finance is permissioned. DeFi is permissionless. Traditional finance discriminates based on geography, wealth, and connections. DeFi treats everyone equally. Traditional finance operates Monday to Friday, 9 to 5. DeFi operates 24/7/365.

The Trust Revolution: From Institutions to Mathematics

The shift from trusting institutions to trusting math is bigger than most people realize. Every aspect of modern society runs on trust. You trust banks to hold your money. Trust governments to maintain currency value. Trust companies to deliver products. Trust courts to enforce contracts.

But trust is fragile. Banks fail. Governments print money. Companies default. Courts can be corrupted. Every point of trust is a point of failure.

Crypto eliminates these trust requirements. You don't trust Bitcoin's monetary policy; you verify it in the code. You don't trust smart contracts to execute; they can't do anything *except* execute. You don't trust DeFi protocols to pay yields; the math ensures it.

This is revolutionary because trust doesn't scale. You can't personally verify every bank's solvency, every government's monetary policy, every company's intentions. So you outsource trust to institutions, regulators, and rating agencies. Who also fail.

But math scales infinitely. The cryptographic proof that secures your Bitcoin works the same whether you have $100 or $100 million. The smart contract that pays your DeFi yield doesn't care who you are or where you're from. Mathematical truth is universal, unchanging, and incorruptible.

We're shifting from a trust-based economy to a verification-based economy. From "Trust me" to "Here's the proof." From institutional promises to mathematical certainties.

Why This Can't Be Stopped

Governments and banks want to stop this revolution. It threatens their monopoly on money creation, financial services, and economic control. But they can't stop math. They can't ban code. They can't un-invent the technology.

China banned Bitcoin mining in 2021. The hash rate dropped briefly, then recovered as miners relocated. The network didn't even hiccup. India banned crypto trading. The Supreme Court overturned it as unconstitutional. Nigeria restricted crypto. Peer-to-peer volume exploded. Every attempt to stop crypto makes it stronger by proving why we need it.

Here's why crypto is unstoppable: *It's decentralized.* There's no CEO to arrest, no company to shut down, no server to seize. Bitcoin nodes run in every country. Ethereum validators span the globe. DeFi protocols exist everywhere and nowhere simultaneously.

It's open-source. The code is public. Anyone can copy it, modify it, improve it. You can't uninvent public knowledge. Even if every government banned crypto tomorrow, the code would survive and evolve.

It's antifragile. Attacks make it stronger. Bear markets shake out weak hands and concentrate ownership among believers. Regulatory crackdowns prove the need for censorship resistance. Every crisis that doesn't kill crypto makes it more resilient.

It's economically inevitable. Countries that ban crypto lose innovators and capital to countries that embrace it. Banks that fight crypto lose customers to banks that integrate it. The economic incentives favor adoption over resistance.

The Emerging Network State

We're not just witnessing new technology. We're watching the birth of network states, digital nations that exist in code rather than geography.

Bitcoin is already a proto-nation. It has citizens (holders), a constitution (the protocol), a monetary policy (the halving schedule), and a defense budget (mining rewards). It provides services (value transfer) and maintains infrastructure (the blockchain). It's more robust than many physical nations.

Ethereum goes further. It's not just a nation but a platform for nations. Thousands of DAOs (decentralized autonomous organizations) operate on Ethereum. They have treasuries and governance systems. They provide services to members. People earn their livings from DAOs, vote on proposals, and build communities. All without traditional corporate or governmental structures.

This isn't science fiction. It's happening now. In part V, we'll explore how to participate in these emerging network states. But understand that we're witnessing something unprecedented: the voluntary formation of digital nations based on shared beliefs rather than geographic accidents.

Your Part in the Revolution

Understanding this revolution transforms you from spectator to participant. You're not just buying tokens; you're joining networks. Not just investing; building new systems. Not just escaping the old; creating the new.

In the coming chapters, we'll build on this foundation. Chapter 5 will dive deep into Bitcoin specifically. Chapter 6 will walk you through your first purchase. Part III will teach you to read markets and build wealth systematically. Part IV will show you how to generate income through DeFi.

But it all starts with understanding what you're actually participating in. This isn't a get-rich-quick scheme or just some fad. It's a fundamental restructuring of how human civilization coordinates, transacts, and creates value.

The printing press democratized information. The internet democratized communication. Blockchain democratizes value and trust. We're living through a revolution as significant as any in history.

The way I see it, either this technology succeeds and rebuilds the global financial system, or it fails and we remain trapped in the current system. There's no middle ground. You can't have "a little bit" of decentralization. You can't be "somewhat" trustless.

And honestly? I can't see a future where this technology doesn't become mainstream. The problems it solves are too fundamental. The inefficiencies it eliminates are too obvious. The freedom it enables is too powerful. Once people experience sending money globally in seconds for pennies, or earning 10% on their savings instead of 0.05%, or accessing financial services without begging for permission, there's no going back.

If you believe the current system is sustainable, that governments will stop printing money, that banks will start serving people over profits, then crypto isn't for you. Keep your savings in fiat and hope for the best.

But if you see what I and millions of others see—a system in terminal decline, a monetary system that's fundamentally broken, a financial system that enriches insiders at everyone else's expense—then you understand why this revolution is inevitable.

The technology exists. The infrastructure is built. The network effects are compounding. Major corporations are adopting it. Countries are making it legal tender. The brightest developers in the world are building on it. This is no longer just speculation about what might happen, but an observation of what's already happening.

The question isn't whether this revolution succeeds. It's whether you'll participate in building the future or watch from the sidelines.

5

Asymmetric Bets:
How Underdogs Turn Small Stakes into Big Wins

5:00 a.m. The sky over Playa del Carmen was still dark, but I couldn't sleep. I was living in Mexico at the time, between businesses, trying to figure out my next move. I had built a 7-figure business but was quickly losing my passion for it, so I was on a bit of a hiatus in that uncomfortable space where you have some money saved but not enough to last long, with no clear direction forward.

This was late 2020, right in the middle of my first crypto bull run. I'd been throwing small amounts at different cryptocurrencies, not really understanding what I was doing but fascinated by the technology and possibility. And if you're anything like me, you'll understand: when I get obsessed with something, I go all in. This wasn't just dabbling. This was full immersion. I was consuming everything I could find about crypto, blockchain, and DeFi from the moment I woke up until 2:00 a.m. YouTube videos played while I brushed my teeth. White papers replaced Netflix. Discord channels buzzed on three monitors while I scribbled notes like a madman.

Most people thought I'd lost it, disappearing into this digital rabbit hole for days at a time. But that's how I've always operated: complete obsession until I understand something at a cellular level. Those months of borderline-unhealthy fixation would later translate into millions of dollars, but at the time I was just a guy in Mexico with too much coffee and not enough sleep, convinced I'd found the future of finance.

That morning, I grabbed my phone and headed to the beach to watch the sunrise, a daily ritual I still do to this day as it helps me think. As I sat on the sand, waiting for the first rays of light, I opened my portfolio app out of habit.

My account was up $8,600. *Overnight. While I was sleeping.*

I refreshed three times, certain it was a glitch. But the numbers held. No team to manage, no client calls to jump on, no sales to close. A bunch of small bets were paying off simultaneously. Bitcoin was up 15%. Ethereum was up 22%. Some random altcoin I'd thrown $200 at was up 400%. Nothing life-changing individually, but together they'd created this moment of clarity.

That morning on the beach, staring at these numbers, I learned about asymmetric bets. Not the term; that would come later. But the concept. The idea that you can risk a little to potentially gain a lot. The idea that small, calculated risks can compound into meaningful wins.

But I learned something else, too, something that would take me years to fully appreciate: the difference between earned income and investment income. I'd just made $8,600 while I was unconscious. No alarm clock. No commute. No clients. No team to manage. No sales calls. And definitely no frozen fingers on an oil rig. My money had worked harder than I ever could, generating returns while I dreamed.

This wasn't just about asymmetric bets. It was about building wealth that compounds without requiring my presence. One type of income needs you to show up every day, trading time for money. The other works 24/7, whether you're sleeping, surfing, or sipping coffee on a Mexican beach. Both have their places, but only one gives you true freedom.

I have to be honest about what happened next, because it's important: I never took profits from that run. I watched what would eventually be over $250,000 of unrealized gains (which was a lot for me back then) evaporate in the 2022 crash. Lost it all, at least on paper. The tuition for that lesson was expensive, but the education was priceless. That lesson alone would help me make millions in the following years. We'll dive deep into profit-taking strategies such as "laddering out" in part III, but know this: paper gains aren't real until you take them.

The Mental Model That Changes Everything

An asymmetric bet is beautifully simple: you risk a little to potentially gain a lot. Your downside is capped, but your upside is wide open. It's the opposite of how most people approach opportunity.

Consider the typical life path. You go to college, taking on $100,000 in debt (massive downside) for the possibility of a decent job (limited upside). You work a job trading irreplaceable time for replaceable money. You save dollars that lose value every year. These are symmetric trades at best, often negatively asymmetric. High risk, limited reward.

Now consider buying $100 worth of Bitcoin or a solid altcoin project. Your maximum loss? $100. Your maximum gain? Theoretically unlimited. Project goes to zero? You lose a nice dinner. Project succeeds? Your $100 becomes thousands. The risk–reward ratio is completely skewed in your favor.

ASYMMETRIC BET

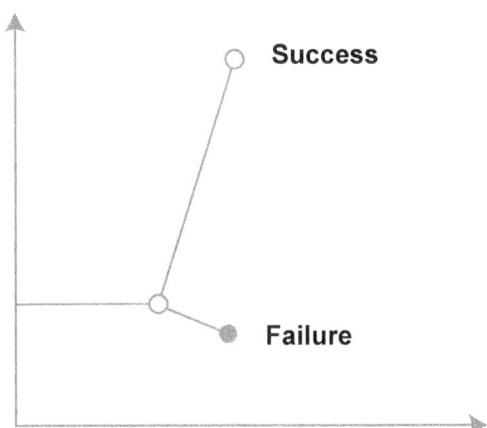

But here's what I discovered after that morning in Mexico: asymmetric bets aren't just about crypto investments. They're a way of thinking about every opportunity in life. And after years of searching for and executing asymmetric bets, I've found they fall into three main categories that anyone can access.

1. **Technology bets** are what brought you to this book. Asymmetric technology bets are investments made in new technology before mass adoption. Bitcoin when everyone thinks it's magic internet money. Ethereum when few understand smart contracts. DeFi protocols before institutional adoption. You're betting that technology that solves real problems will eventually be understood and valued by the masses.

The key is distinguishing genuine innovation from hype. Real asymmetric technology bets solve real problems for real people. When you find technology that makes you think, "Why doesn't everyone see this?", that's often your asymmetric opportunity. That's exactly how I felt when I discovered DeFi could pay me 8% on stablecoins while banks were offering 0.05% on fiat.

2. **Business bets** are the most accessible form of asymmetry. Starting a business costs time and maybe a few thousand dollars, but the upside is unlimited. My YouTube channel, CryptoLabs Research (www.youtube.com/@cryptolabsresearch), started with a $100 microphone and a few embarrassing first videos. That tiny YouTube channel eventually brought me multiple 7-figure opportunities, investments, and multiple sources of income. The beautiful thing about asymmetric business bets? Even failure pays dividends. Every failed business teaches you skills, builds your network, increases your odds of success next time.

3. **Skill bets** might be the most undervalued category of asymmetric betting. Learning high-value skills costs time and maybe money for courses, but the returns compound forever. To date, I've invested over $500,000 in courses, coaching, and masterminds, and that investment has returned over 20x. When you learn to understand blockchain, use DeFi, or read market cycles, these skills multiply the value of everything else you do. The downside is focused learning time. The upside is a permanent increase in earning potential.

Now, all that said, not everything claiming to be asymmetric actually is. Sometimes it's hard to spot the difference. Here's the framework I use:

First, calculate the real downside. Not just money, but time, opportunity cost, reputation. Can you afford a total loss? If the loss would significantly impact your life, the bet is too large. Size accordingly.

Second, assess realistic upside. Ignore hype and marketing. What's the genuine potential based on comparable examples? Look for opportunities where even moderate success provides 5x or higher returns.

Third, consider probability of success. A lottery ticket is technically asymmetric, but probability is near zero. Good asymmetric bets have reasonable success probability with massive payoffs when they hit. I can't see a future where crypto's market cap is smaller than today, so I place my bets accordingly.

Fourth, factor in timeline. Can you wait long enough for asymmetry to play out? Bitcoin's asymmetry took years to manifest. If you need returns quickly, long-term asymmetric bets won't work.

Finally, evaluate educational value. The best asymmetric bets teach you regardless of outcome. Even if the investment fails, do you gain knowledge, skills, or connections that make future bets more likely to succeed?

My Six-Figure Lesson in False Asymmetry

Let me tell you about Terra Luna—not to scare you off, but because understanding false asymmetry is as important as recognizing real opportunity.

Terra Luna was an algorithmic stablecoin project that promised the impossible: a decentralized dollar that maintained its value through code and incentives rather than actual dollar reserves. UST (TerraUSD) was supposed to always equal $1, maintained through a complex minting and burning mechanism with LUNA tokens. When UST dropped below $1, you could burn it to mint $1 worth of LUNA, creating arbitrage that should have restored the peg. When UST went above $1, the opposite happened.

The system offered 20% yields through something called anchor protocol. Twenty percent annual returns on a "stablecoin" seemed perfect: low risk, high reward. I took most of the profits from the business I was running and put over $200,000 into Terra Luna, convinced I'd found the holy grail. Thousands of others thought the same. We were all wrong.

Looking back now, it's obvious it was unsustainable. The yield came from token emissions, not real economic activity. The mechanism required constant new money to maintain. The whole thing was a house of cards. But I didn't have a book like this to help me spot the warning signs. I had to learn through expensive failure what you can learn through these pages.

In May 2022, the entire system collapsed in just 72 hours. A large withdrawal triggered a depeg. The arbitrage mechanism that was supposed to save the system instead created a death spiral. People burned UST for LUNA, causing massive LUNA inflation. More LUNA supply meant lower LUNA price. Lower LUNA price meant the mechanism couldn't defend the peg. UST fell to $0.10. One LUNA, which had been $80, went to essentially zero. The profits I'd worked years to build were gone in three days.

This taught me the crucial difference between real and false asymmetry. Terra Luna wasn't asymmetric; it was binary. All or nothing. Either the mechanism worked forever (impossible) or it failed catastrophically (inevitable). True asymmetric bets have multiple ways to win and limited, defined downsides. Bitcoin can appreciate through adoption, store of value narrative, or currency use. Terra Luna had one mechanism that would either work or destroy everything.

But here's the key lesson: that loss was only part of my crypto portfolio. Even in my greed, I'd maintained position sizing. The loss hurt tremendously, both financially and emotionally. Watching years of business profits evaporate was devastating. But my other asymmetric bets (Bitcoin, Ethereum, quality DeFi protocols) more than covered it. That's the power of portfolio construction. When you're wrong on one position, you lose 1x. When you're right on others, you gain 10x, 50x, or more.

The Terra Luna collapse taught me to always ask: where does the yield come from? If the answer requires complex explanations about tokenomics and incentives rather than simple value creation, it's probably unsustainable. Real yield comes from real economic activity: trading fees, lending interest, and actual usage. Fake yield comes from token printing that eventually collapses.

Your Asymmetric Portfolio Blueprint

Building wealth through asymmetric bets requires structure, not gambling. We'll dive much deeper into portfolio construction in Part III, but here's the framework to get you started:

First. calculate your asymmetric budget. Use money you won't need for 2+ years. Whether $500 or $500,000, the timeline matters more than the amount. If losing it affects your sleep or ability to pay bills, it's too much.

The allocation I've refined over years of expensive mistakes starts with 50% (or more; it could be up to 100%) in core assets: Bitcoin and Ethereum. These form your foundation that won't ever return 100x again, but also won't go to zero. They're the bedrock upon which you build everything else.

Up to 30% goes into emerging narratives, the next wave of innovation before it becomes obvious. Currently that means DeFi protocols with real revenue, Layer 2s that solve scalability, and intersection plays such as AI meeting crypto. These carry 10–50x potential while being established enough to avoid total collapse. By the time you read this book, that may have changed, but we'll dive into how to find these opportunities for yourself later in this book.

Then you can allocate up to 15% to early-stage plays, focusing on smaller caps with real usage, not memecoins or hype projects. These are protocols that solve actual problems and haven't been discovered by the masses yet. The asymmetry here is beautiful: you might lose everything or gain 1,000%.

The final 5%, if you need to scratch the itch, goes to moonshots, your lottery tickets. Most will fail completely, but one 100x in this category pays for all failures and then some. Never put more than 5% here, because these are pure speculation.

If you want an even simpler guideline, follow the barbell strategy: 80% in established assets, 20% in higher-risk opportunities. The barbell strategy helps concentrate most of your capital in ultra-safe, long-term assets while reserving a small portion for high-upside, asymmetric opportunities. The exact ratio depends on your stage and conviction. It might start as 80/20, evolve to 90/10, or even 95/5, but the principle stays the same. For every position you take, document your thesis. Write down why you believe in it, what would invalidate that belief, and when you'll reassess. This prevents emotional decisions and ensures you learn from both wins and losses. When Terra Luna collapsed, my documentation helped me understand exactly what warning signs I'd missed.

The key principle driving all of this: you're not trying to be right every time. You're positioning so that when you're right, it pays for all the times you're wrong plus massive profit. Think like a venture capitalist who expects 90% of bets to fail but needs just one unicorn to make the fund.

We'll expand on each of these components in part III, including specific rebalancing strategies, risk management, and quality project assessment checklists.

Three Asymmetric Bets You Can Make Today

Theory without action is worthless. You've learned why the system is broken and how crypto provides the escape route. Now it's time to take your first real steps into this new financial system. Here are three specific actions you can take within the next 48 hours that perfectly demonstrate asymmetric risk–reward.

Start by reading the Bitcoin white paper if you haven't already. Go to bitcoin. org and find it. Nine pages that changed the world. It'll be confusing at first; maybe you'll understand 10% on your initial read. That's completely normal. This isn't about full comprehension yet; it's about beginning your education with the source document that started everything. Your downside is an hour of reading something technical. Your upside is beginning to understand the foundation of a multi-trillion dollar revolution. Grasping even 10% of it will put you ahead of 99% of people who own crypto but have never read the document that created it.

Next, open an account on Coinbase, Kraken, or Binance and buy your first $100 of Bitcoin. Start the verification today, since it might take 24–48 hours. Once approved, buy exactly $100 worth. Not $50 because you're scared, not $500 because you're excited. Exactly $100. We'll dive deeper into the differences between centralized exchanges like these and decentralized exchanges in chapter 7, but for now, don't worry about it. These platforms are the simplest on-ramp from dollars to crypto, and that's all you need right now.

This $100 is the perfect amount because it gets you into the game but not enough to hurt if anything goes wrong. Your maximum downside is the cost of a nice dinner. Your upside? You now have skin in the game. You'll start seeing Fed announcements differently. You'll understand viscerally what owning uncensorable money feels like (especially once you move it to cold storage, which we'll be talking about shortly). Most importantly, having real money at stake transforms how you learn. Reading about Bitcoin is education. Owning Bitcoin is transformation. If you don't yet own any Bitcoin, the next chapter will walk you through every step of this process.

Finally, invest an hour or two in real education. Watch 10 videos from our CryptoLabs Research YouTube channel (https://youtube.com/@cryptolabsresearch), where we break down markets, strategies, and concepts in plain English. Then jump on DeFiBuddy.io and spend time exploring the crypto ecosystem. Don't invest anything yet; just explore. Look at different projects and their market caps. Check out what protocols exist beyond Bitcoin. See what kinds of yields are available in DeFi. Start getting familiar with the landscape.

Your downside here is two hours of time. Your upside is unlimited. You'll start recognizing patterns, understanding terminology, and seeing opportunities. You'll go from complete outsider to informed beginner in one focused session. The people making millions in crypto all started exactly where you are now, spending a few hours trying to understand this new world.

The beauty of these three bets is their asymmetry. Combined, you're risking $100 and a few hours. That's less than a night out. But the potential upsides include understanding the future of money, participating in the greatest wealth transfer in history, and developing knowledge that could transform your financial future. Even if Bitcoin goes to zero (it won't), the education and paradigm shift alone are worth multiples of your investment.

The Compound Effect of Asymmetric Thinking

Once you train your brain to see asymmetric opportunities, the world transforms into an endless source of favorable bets. Every decision gets filtered through this new lens. Should you keep your savings in a bank account where it loses 7% annually to inflation, or learn about stablecoin yields earning

10%? Should you accept that traditional finance is "how things work," or invest time understanding the alternative being built?

This mental shift compounds because asymmetric thinkers attract asymmetric opportunities. When you start taking calculated risks and documenting the results, people notice. You become someone who acts rather than debates. Your network expands to include others playing the same game. You stop competing with the masses trading time for money and start collaborating with builders creating exponential value.

My entire life transformed not when I made my first profitable investment, but when I started filtering every decision through the asymmetric lens. That morning on that beach in Mexico, watching my portfolio up $8,600 overnight, I learned something worth more than any gains: when you structure bets properly, you don't need to be right often. You just need to be right occasionally with proper position sizing.

Up Next...

We've spent these first five chapters demolishing the lies you've been told about money and revealing the escape route. You now understand why the system that interrogates you for accessing your own money is optional. You know why Bitcoin isn't just internet money but a complete reconstruction of what money can be. You see how every dollar in savings is melting ice, losing value by design. You grasp the technology enabling an entirely new financial system. And you understand the mental model that turns small bets into life-changing outcomes.

Part II will transform you from observer to participant. Part III will teach you to read markets like a native. Part IV will show you how to generate income that seems impossible to anyone mired in traditional finance. And part V will tackle the more important piece of all: your investor mindset. But everything starts with taking action on the asymmetric opportunities in front of you right now.

You don't need wealth to start. You don't need permission. You don't need credentials. You just need the courage to bet on yourself when the odds are actually, mathematically in your favor. The market doesn't wait. Opportunity doesn't pause. But now, armed with the asymmetric mindset, you're ready to stop watching and start building.

Onward we go!

Part II:

Crypto Wealth Foundations

6

Your First $100 in Crypto
(Without Getting Scammed)

The hardest step in crypto isn't understanding the technology or mastering trading strategies. It's the first one: *actually putting real money into this new system*. Your brain will generate a thousand reasons to wait: The price might drop. You might lose it all. You don't understand enough yet. These fears are natural and even rational as you're moving money from a system you know to one you're still learning.

You'll never feel 100% ready. There will never be a perfect time. The price will never feel "right." Every successful crypto investor started exactly where you are now, uncertain but willing to begin. They didn't wait for complete understanding. They started small, learned by doing, and built confidence through experience. Every day you wait is opportunity cost accumulating. The best time to start was yesterday. The second best time is now.

This chapter walks you through your first crypto purchase step by step. No complex strategies. No overwhelming choices. Just the simplest path from fiat to your first satoshi. We'll visit more advanced strategies in later chapters, but let's start with the basics.

Choosing Your First Exchange

Exchanges are the bridges between traditional money and crypto. They're not ideal, and we'll discuss why you shouldn't keep coins there long-term, but they're necessary for converting dollars to Bitcoin.

For your first purchase, stick with established centralized exchanges (CEXs). Yes, I know this contradicts the decentralization ethos, and yes, we'll move to decentralized exchanges (DEXs) later. But for your very first purchase, you need simplicity and reliability.

The Big Three for Beginners

Coinbase is the training wheels of crypto. Most user-friendly interface, best educational resources, insured holdings up to $250,000. The downside? Higher fees (up to 4% for simple buys). Think of it as paying for simplicity and peace of mind on your first purchase.

Kraken offers lower fees (around 1.5%) with slightly more complexity. Better for those comfortable with basic trading interfaces. Excellent security track record, never been hacked since 2011 launch. My personal favorite for beginners who can handle a small learning curve.

Binance has the most options and the lowest fees (0.1% with BNB), but it can overwhelm beginners. The Walmart of crypto—everything you could want, but it's easy to get lost. Save this for when you're comfortable with the basics.

Beyond these three, there are dozens more exchanges: Gemini with its focus on regulation and security, KuCoin with extensive altcoin selections, Crypto.com with their aggressive marketing and card rewards, Bybit for derivatives trading, Newton for Canadians, and many others. Each has its pros and cons, different fee structures, and varying coin selections. You could spend weeks researching the perfect exchange, comparing fee schedules, and reading reviews. But here's the truth: for your first $100 Bitcoin purchase, it doesn't matter that much. Pick one of the big three based on your comfort level with complexity versus fees, and just start. You can always open accounts on other exchanges later as you learn what you prefer. Also remember we'll rarely be using centralized exchanges, so don't worry too much about any of this for now.

The Account Setup Process

The verification process will feel invasive. Photo ID, proof of address, sometimes video verification. You'll wonder why buying "decentralized" currency requires so much personal information.

This isn't the exchange being difficult; it's government regulation requiring "know your customer" (KYC) compliance. The irony of needing permission to buy permissionless money isn't lost on anyone. But this is the current reality of on-ramps from fiat to crypto.

Start the verification process today, even if you're not ready to buy. It often takes 24–72 hours to get approved. While you're waiting, you can continue learning. When you're ready to buy, the door is already open.

Pro tip: Use your actual information. Don't try to be clever with fake names or addresses. Exchanges share blacklists, and getting banned from one can mean getting banned from all. Plus, you'll need this for tax purposes later.

Your First Purchase: Keep It Simple

For your first purchase, I recommend starting with $100–$500. Enough that you care, not so much that losing it would affect your life. This isn't your retirement fund. It's your education fund.

Log into your chosen exchange. Navigate to the buy section. You'll see options that might overwhelm you: market orders, limit orders, stop losses, margins. Ignore all of that for now.

Choose "Simple Buy" or "Instant Buy" (terminology varies by exchange). Select Bitcoin for your first purchase. Yes, there are thousands of other options. Yes, some random altcoin might go 100x tomorrow. But Bitcoin is the foundation everything else builds on. Start here.

Enter your dollar amount. The exchange will calculate how much Bitcoin that will get you at the current price. The number will seem small, like 0.0025

BTC. That's normal. You're not buying whole coins; you're buying fractions called satoshis.

Review the fees. Expect to pay 1–4% for simple purchases. On a $100 purchase, that's $1–4. Yes, it's higher than you'd like. Consider it tuition for entering the new financial system. Once you're more experienced, you can optimize fees using limit orders and advanced features. Plus, once you get into DeFi, you'll pay pennies instead of dollars.

Click buy. Take a breath. Congratulations. You've just done what 95% of people talking about crypto have never done. You've actually participated instead of just speculating.

After Your First Purchase: Resist the Urge

Your immediate urge will be to stare at the price. You'll refresh obsessively, calculating your gains or losses on every 1% movement. When Bitcoin moves 5%, your $100 becoming $105 or $95 will feel massive.

This is normal but unproductive. Instead, use this energy to learn. Set up price alerts so you don't need to check constantly. Join communities where you can discuss what you're learning (we have a free course and community you can join at www.CryptolabsResearch.com). Start researching wallet options for getting your Bitcoin off the exchange.

Your second urge will be to tell everyone. Resist this, too. Not because crypto is shameful, but because most people aren't ready to hear it. They'll either mock you for gambling or suddenly become your financial advisor. Neither is helpful. Find communities of people already in crypto with whom to share your journey.

Common First-Timer Mistakes to Avoid

After watching thousands of people make their first crypto purchase through our community, I've seen the same painful mistakes repeated over and over. Learn from their expensive lessons so you don't have to pay the same tuition to the market.

The most common mistake is FOMO buying during pumps. Picture this: Bitcoin has been quietly trading at $60,000 for weeks, and you're still "researching" whether to buy. Then suddenly it rockets to $72,000 in three days. The media starts covering it. Your coworker mentions their gains. Twitter is nothing but rocket emojis. That fear of missing out becomes overwhelming, and you finally pull the trigger at the exact moment everyone else is euphoric. Two days later, it corrects back to $65,000 and you're immediately down 10%. This isn't bad luck; it's bad timing driven by emotion instead of strategy. For your first $100 purchase, I wouldn't worry too much about it. Plus we are investing for the long term, so there really is no need to try and time the markets. More about that later in the book.

The opposite mistake is equally costly: trying to time the perfect bottom. I know people who wanted to buy Bitcoin at $20,000 in 2020. They waited for it to drop to $15,000. It went to $30,000 instead. They decided to wait for the correction back to $20,000. It went to $60,000. They're still waiting, now that it's over $100,000, having missed a 5x gain because they wanted to save 25% on their entry. The perfect entry doesn't exist. Always remember that time in the market beats timing the market, especially in an asset that's appreciated an average of 200% annually over the past decade.

Another expensive error is buying random altcoins for your first purchase. You see Bitcoin at $100,000 and think it's "too expensive," then notice pumpcoin at $0.08 and think it's "cheap." This is like saying a single Amazon share at $3,000 is more expensive than 3,000 shares of a penny stock. Price per coin means nothing; market cap and quality mean everything. More about that later, but your first purchase should be Bitcoin or Ethereum, period. Not some micro cap that your friend's cousin swears will 100x. Not the meme-coin that's trending on social media. Start with the assets that have survived multiple cycles and proven themselves. You can explore altcoins later when you understand what you're buying.

The mistake that causes the most pain is investing more than you can afford to lose. Your first purchase is an experiment in a volatile asset class. If you invest rent money, you'll panic-sell the first time it drops 20%. If you use credit cards, you're paying 20% interest to invest in something that might drop 50% before recovering. If you touch your emergency fund, you may be forced to sell at the worst possible time when life inevitably throws you a curve ball. Only invest what you can watch go to zero without it affecting your ability to pay bills, sleep at night, or maintain relationships.

Finally, there's the mistake that turns temporary losses into permanent ones: panic-selling on the first dip. Bitcoin moves 10% regularly, sometimes in a single day. Your $100 investment might be worth $90 tomorrow morning and $110 by dinner. This isn't a crisis; it's Tuesday in crypto. These movements that would constitute a crash in stock markets are normal volatility here. If you can't handle watching your investment swing 10% without breaking into a cold sweat, you've invested too much. Size your position so that you can watch it drop 20% without losing sleep, because that might happen, and historically, those who held and accumulated through those drops were rewarded handsomely.

The pattern is always the same with new investors. They research for months, finally buy at a local peak driven by FOMO, watch it immediately drop 15%, panic-sell at a loss, then watch it recover and go higher, buy back in higher than they sold, and repeat this expensive dance until they call Bitcoin a scam. Don't be part of this statistic. Make your first purchase with money you've written off mentally, expect volatility, and give it at least a full year before judging whether it was a good decision.

Remember, everyone who got wealthy in crypto went through these same emotional challenges. The difference between those who succeeded and those who failed wasn't intelligence or timing; it was the ability to stick to a plan despite emotional pressure. Make your plan before you buy, when you're calm and rational, then follow it regardless of what the market or your emotions tell you later.

Building From Your First $100

Your first purchase is just the beginning. It's proof you can do this. From here, you can build systematically. Consider dollar cost averaging (DCA). Instead of trying to time the market, buy a fixed dollar amount weekly or monthly. It could be $25 every Monday, or $100 every first of the month. This averages your entry price over time and removes emotion from the decision.

What is Dollar-Cost Averaging?

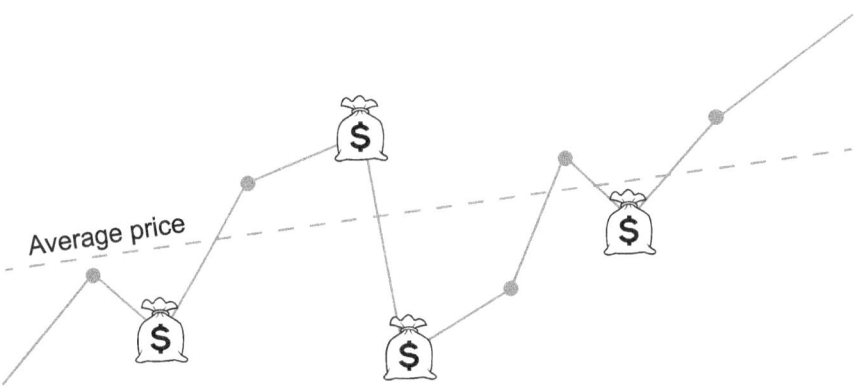

Average price

Start learning about other assets. Once comfortable with Bitcoin, research Ethereum. Understand the difference between proof of work and proof of stake. Learn about smart contracts and DeFi. But don't rush. Master one thing before moving to the next. This book is laid out in a way that will take you from beginner (or wherever you're at) to pro in 26 chapters.

Track your purchases and reasoning. Keep a simple spreadsheet: date, amount, price, and why you bought. This creates a record of your thinking that you can learn from. Were you buying from FOMO or strategy? Did your reasoning prove correct?

Also, that first $100 purchase changes you in ways you don't expect. You start perceiving financial news differently. Fed announcements matter because they affect your Bitcoin. Inflation reports become personal. You develop opinions about monetary policy.

You also start thinking in longer timeframes. Traditional investors think in quarters. Crypto investors think in cycles. Your $100 might be $90 in a month but $500 in a year and $5,000 in five years. This long-term thinking extends beyond investing into life planning.

Most importantly, you've broken the inertia. The hardest part of any journey is the first step. Once you've bought your first Bitcoin, the second purchase is easier. Learning wallets becomes necessary, not theoretical. Understanding DeFi becomes interesting, not overwhelming.

Your Next Steps

After your first purchase, your education accelerates. You have skin in the game now. Every concept matters more when you have money at stake. You're in the arena!

Next up, chapter 7 explores the critical difference between centralized and decentralized exchanges, explaining why CEXs are necessary evils for fiat conversion but terrible for storage, while DEXs offer true freedom but require more knowledge.

Chapter 8 covers the most important lesson in crypto: taking custody of your coins. You'll learn why leaving crypto on exchanges is like leaving cash with strangers who keep going bankrupt, and how hardware wallets give you uncensorable ownership of your wealth.

Chapter 9 demystifies Ethereum and smart contracts without requiring a computer science degree. You'll understand how Ethereum enables programmable money and why this matters for everything that comes next.

Chapter 10 teaches essential security measures that will save you from joining the countless people who've lost everything because of preventable mistakes. You'll learn to spot scams, secure your assets, and navigate the crypto space safely.

From there, part III teaches you to master the markets like a native, not a tourist. You'll understand the four-year cycles that create millionaires, learn why HODLing beats trading 95% of the time, and discover how to read market psychology so well that your own emotions become your best indicator. Most importantly, you'll master the art of actually taking profits instead of watching gains evaporate, and you'll build a portfolio architecture that survives 80% crashes while positioning you for 1000% gains.

Part IV shows you how to become your own bank through DeFi, earning the yields banks used to monopolize. You'll learn to provide liquidity and earn from every trade, understand impermanent loss so panic doesn't destroy your positions, and discover concentrated liquidity strategies that can 10x your capital efficiency. We'll explore Layer 2s, where transactions cost pennies instead of hundreds, and master velocity strategies that make one dollar work like ten.

Finally, part V transforms your mindset from that of an employee to that of an investor. You'll find your "why" that's stronger than any bear market, understand the J-curve of why everything gets worse before it gets exponentially better, and learn the wealth principles that separate the rich from everyone else. This psychological transformation is what separates those who dabble from those who build generational wealth.

But none of that knowledge matters until you take the first step. Open that exchange account today. Start the verification process. When approved, make that first purchase. Even if it's just $100. The revolution isn't waiting, and neither should you.

7

Permission vs. Freedom:
Why Crypto Is the Exit Door

May 2022. Terra Luna was collapsing in real time. UST, the "stablecoin" that wasn't stable, was depegging from the dollar. I watched my position crater and knew I had to act fast.

I had USDT on Terra that needed liquidating immediately. Every second counted as the ecosystem imploded around me. I transferred everything to my centralized exchange account to swap it for something, anything, that might hold value.

That's when the screen flashed red: "Account temporarily restricted due to suspicious activity."

Suspicious activity? I was trying to save my own money from a collapsing protocol. But the exchange's algorithm had flagged the sudden volume as suspicious. Now I needed their permission to access my own funds during the most critical moment.

The customer service nightmare that followed was surreal. Upload documents. Explain the source of funds. Wait for review. Meanwhile, I watched helplessly as my holdings, which had been worth well over $250K, spiraled quickly toward zero. By the time Terra graciously restored my account access, my holdings were close to worthless.

That's the day I learned the brutal difference between centralized and decentralized exchanges. One requires permission. The other just requires your wallet.

CEX vs. DEX: The Fundamental Difference

You just made your first purchase in chapter 6, probably on Coinbase or another centralized exchange. That was the right move for your first buy. But now you need to understand what you're actually using and why there's something fundamentally different waiting.

A centralized exchange like Coinbase, Binance, or Kraken is just a traditional company with servers, employees, and bank accounts. When you trade on a CEX, you're not really trading crypto. You're trading IOUs within their database. They hold all the actual crypto in their wallets. You're trusting them to honor your balance when you want to withdraw. *You don't actually hold or own your Bitcoin.*

This trust comes with consequences. They can freeze your account for any reason or no reason. They can be hacked, and your funds disappear. They can gamble with customer deposits, like FTX did. They can go bankrupt, and you become an unsecured creditor. They require your personal information, report to governments, and decide what you can and can't trade.

A decentralized exchange is completely different. There's no company. No servers to hack. No employees to bribe. No CEO to run off with funds. A DEX is just smart contract code running on the blockchain.

When you trade on Uniswap, for example, your crypto never leaves your wallet until the moment of the trade. You connect your wallet, you approve the transaction, and the smart contract swaps your tokens directly. No permission needed. No account to freeze. No KYC documents. No waiting for approval while your portfolio burns.

If Terra had happened while I was using a DEX, I would have swapped instantly. No algorithm flagging my activity. No customer service hold. No begging for permission to save my own money. Just connect, swap, done.

The Hidden Cost of "Free" Trading

Centralized exchanges love advertising "zero fees" or "low fees," but that's marketing sleight of hand. They make their money on the *spread*, aka the difference between buy and sell prices. When you buy Bitcoin on Coinbase, you're not getting the real market price. You're getting *their* price, which includes a hidden markup.

I've tracked this personally. Buying $10,000 of Bitcoin on a major CEX with a "0.5% fee" actually costs about 2–3% or more when you factor in the spread. That's $200–300 in hidden costs. Selling tells the same story. Round trip, you're losing 4–6% just to the exchange.

DEXs are transparent about costs. You see exactly what you're paying (usually 0.3% per swap on major pairs). No hidden spreads. No mysterious price differences. The price you see is the price you get, minus the clearly stated fee.

But here's where it gets interesting. Those DEX fees? They don't go to some company's profit margin. They go to liquidity providers, regular people like you and me who deposit their tokens into pools that enable trading.

Becoming the Exchange Instead of Using It

This is the mind-blowing part that connects to everything we'll explore in the DeFi chapters: on a DEX, you can *be* the exchange and earn those fees yourself.

When you provide liquidity to a DEX, you're supplying the tokens that enable others to trade. Every time someone swaps tokens using your liquidity, you earn a portion of the trading fees. Instead of paying fees to Coinbase's shareholders, you're earning fees as a liquidity provider.

I have positions in several DEX liquidity pools right now. Every trade that happens, I get a cut. It's not massive on each trade, maybe 0.01%, but it adds up. Thousands of trades daily, compounding over months. I'm earning the fees that centralized exchanges used to monopolize.

Think about that. Not only can you trade without permission on a DEX, you can actually become part of the infrastructure and earn from it. Try becoming a part-owner of Coinbase and earning from their trading fees. Unless you're buying their stock (which pays no dividend), you can't.

Privacy as a Human Right

Every CEX demands your life story. Government ID. Proof of address. Source of funds. Employment information. They track every trade, report to tax authorities, and share your data with whoever asks nicely (or not so nicely).

I get it. They're complying with regulations. They don't have a choice if they want to operate legally. But that's exactly the point. They're companies that can be pressured, regulated, and controlled. Your financial privacy becomes collateral damage in their compliance.

DEXs don't know who you are and don't care. Your wallet address isn't tied to your identity. You can trade what you want, when you want, without explaining yourself to anyone. This isn't about doing anything shady. It's about privacy being a human right.

The irony is thick: crypto was created to separate money from state control, but CEXs reintroduce all the surveillance and control that crypto was meant to eliminate. It's like inventing the airplane and then using it only to taxi on highways.

The Liquidity Evolution

Early DEXs had a problem: liquidity. Without market makers and order books, how do you ensure there's always someone to trade with? The answer revolutionized not just exchanges but all of DeFi.

Automated Market Makers (AMMs) solved this problem by creating liquidity pools. There's no need to match buyers with sellers; instead, trades happen against pools of tokens. The ratio of tokens in the pool determines the price. Simple, elegant, and it doesn't require any central coordinator. Don't worry too much about this for now; we have an entire chapter dedicated to this in part 4.

This innovation means DEXs can list any token instantly. No approval process. No listing fees. No gatekeepers deciding what you can trade. If someone creates a liquidity pool, that token is tradable. This democratization of market creation is why innovation happens so fast in crypto. Anyone can launch a token and create a market for it in minutes.

The Reality of DEXs Today: Why Most People Still Use CEXs

The truth is that despite all the benefits of decentralized exchanges, the vast majority of crypto investors still rely heavily on centralized platforms. Understanding why reveals both the current limitations and the massive opportunity ahead.

Network fees on Ethereum mainnet vary with activity but have historically been a barrier for smaller traders. During the 2021 bull market's peak congestion, fees temporarily spiked to extreme levels—I once paid $300 in total fees just to set up a single liquidity position. While mainnet fees have since normalized and typically range from $5–20 for complex operations, they can still spike during high-demand periods, making it at times impractical for trades under $1,000.

This is where Layer 2 solutions have changed everything. The same swap that might cost $20 on mainnet costs $0.50 on Arbitrum or Base. DEXs often require multiple transactions: approving tokens, executing swaps, adding liquidity. On Layer 2s, all of these combined might cost $2 total, making DeFi accessible to everyone, not just whales.

The user experience on a DEX remains significantly more complex than that typical of centralized exchanges. On Coinbase, you click "buy" and you're done. On a DEX, you need to connect your wallet, ensure you have ETH for gas, approve token spending, set slippage tolerance, and potentially deal with failed transactions. Each step has multiple points of potential confusion. Send tokens to the wrong address on a CEX, and support might help you. Send them to the wrong address on a DEX, and they're gone forever with no recourse.

Liquidity on a DEX remains fragmented compared to centralized venues. While major pairs like ETH/USDC have deep liquidity, smaller tokens might face 5–10% slippage on any significant trade. CEXs often have tighter spreads and deeper order books, especially for less-popular tokens.

But these aren't fundamental flaws; they're growing pains of revolutionary technology. Layer 2 solutions have already reduced fees from $100 to $0.10. Account abstraction is making wallets as easy as traditional apps. Aggregators are solving liquidity fragmentation by routing trades across multiple DEXs automatically. The gap between CEX and DEX user experiences shrinks daily while the freedom gap widens exponentially.

After years of navigating both systems and losing money to both CEX failures and DEX mistakes, I've developed a practical approach. Centralized exchanges have exactly one legitimate use case: converting between fiat and crypto. You can't deposit dollars to Uniswap or withdraw USD from a DEX. CEXs are the necessary bridge between old and new money.

Think of CEXs like border checkpoints between countries. You don't live at the checkpoint; you pass through as quickly as possible. When I need to buy crypto with fiat, I deposit the exact amount I plan to convert, make the purchase immediately, and withdraw everything to my hardware wallet within minutes. The entire process takes less than an hour. For selling, I send only what I'm converting to fiat, sell it, and withdraw the fiat immediately.

Never store on a CEX. Never hold on one. Never trust one. Just use it as the on/off ramp it should be. Everything else happens on DEXs, where your funds remain in your control. Yes, the learning curve is steeper. Yes, mistakes are more costly. But the alternative is trusting companies that have repeatedly proven they can't be trusted with your money.

The future is clear: DEXs will dominate as Layer 2s eliminate gas fees (the fee you pay for a transaction) and interfaces become intuitive. CEXs will remain as regulated fiat gateways, nothing more. Position yourself on the right side of this transition by learning DEX mechanics now, while most people still cling to the familiar danger of centralized platforms.

The Regulatory Storm Coming

CEXs are getting squeezed from both sides. Governments want more control, more reporting, more restrictions. Users want more freedom, more privacy, more access. These demands are fundamentally incompatible.

We're already seeing the results. Binance banned in multiple countries. Coinbase fighting the SEC. Kraken delisting privacy coins. Every month, CEXs become more restrictive, less useful, more like the traditional banks they were supposed to replace.

Meanwhile, DEXs can't be regulated in the same way. There's no company to sue, no servers to seize, no CEO to arrest. You can ban the website, but the smart contracts live on the blockchain.

This isn't about being anti-regulation or anti-government. It's about recognizing that permissionless systems can't be turned into permissioned ones without destroying what makes them valuable.

With all that said, DEXs are evolving rapidly. Layer 2 solutions make trades nearly free and instant. New innovations like concentrated liquidity make capital more efficient. Cross-chain bridges enable trading across different blockchains. Limit orders, perpetuals, options, every financial instrument is being rebuilt in decentralized form.

Meanwhile, CEXs are becoming more restrictive, more regulated, more likely to freeze your funds for compliance reviews. The gap in user experience is closing, while the gap in freedom is widening.

The writing is on the wall. Centralized exchanges are the past. They're necessary (for now) bridges to the old financial system, but ultimately they're incompatible with crypto's vision of permissionless finance. DEXs are the future, where code replaces companies and math replaces trust.

Lessons Learned the Hard Way

My painful lesson during Terra's collapse taught me what everyone eventually learns: when you need your money most, centralized exchanges will fail you.

Not might fail you. Will fail you. Through malice, incompetence, or just bad timing, they will eventually let you down when it matters.

The choice between CEX and DEX isn't about convenience or features. It's about permission versus freedom. It's about trusting companies versus trusting code. It's about being a customer versus being sovereign.

Every trade you make on a DEX is a vote for the future of finance. Every fee you earn as a liquidity provider is proof that we don't need traditional exchanges. The infrastructure exists. Billions of dollars' worth of liquidity is there for a reason. The only question is whether you'll keep asking for permission or start taking your freedom.

8

Not Your Keys, Not Your Coins: How to Actually Own Your Wealth

So you've bought some Bitcoin. You understand it's the soundest form of money ever created. You're excited about financial sovereignty. But, as you learned in the last chapter, if that Bitcoin is sitting on Coinbase, Binance, or any other exchange, you don't own Bitcoin. You own an IOU for Bitcoin. And now that you understand the difference between CEXs and DEXs, let's focus on the most important lesson in crypto: actually taking control of your assets.

Holding crypto on an exchange is no better than holding dollars in a bank. Actually, it might be worse. At least banks have FDIC insurance up to $250,000. When crypto exchanges fail, and many have, you become an "unsecured creditor" fighting for scraps in bankruptcy court.

The entire point of Bitcoin is removing intermediaries. Eliminating trust requirements. Taking control of your own wealth. But if you're leaving your coins on an exchange, you've just replaced Bank of America with Binance. Different master, same slavery.

This chapter completes your journey to true ownership. Because until you hold your own keys, those coins aren't actually yours.

The Graveyard of Broken Promises

We need to talk about exchange failures, because until you understand the scale of destruction, you won't take custody seriously.

Mt. Gox (2014): The original disaster. This exchange handled 70% of all Bitcoin transactions worldwide. Everyone trusted it. Then 850,000 Bitcoin vanished. The exchange had been insolvent for years, using new deposits to pay withdrawals. Customers are still in court a decade later, fighting for 20% of their Bitcoin's 2014 value. Those 850,000 Bitcoin would be worth $85 billion today.

QuadrigaCX (2019): Canada's largest exchange. The founder died (or so it is claimed; not everyone is convinced) in India with sole access to cold wallets. $190 million gone. Investigation revealed he'd been running a Ponzi scheme, gambling customer funds on other exchanges. The cold wallets had been empty long before his mysterious death.

Celsius (2022): "Unbank yourself" was their slogan. They promised sustainable yields while secretly gambling deposits. When crypto prices dropped, they froze withdrawals overnight. No warning. The bankruptcy revealed a $1.2 billion hole. CEO withdrew $10 million before the freeze. Customers are still waiting for pennies on the dollar.

FTX (2022): The one that hurt most. Sam Bankman-Fried was supposed to be different. Tom Brady and Steph Curry in Super Bowl ads. The "safe, regulated" choice. Behind the scenes, customer deposits went to Alameda Research for gambling. When withdrawals spiked, $8 billion was missing.

Every exchange is susceptible to failure through malice, incompetence, regulation, or circumstances. The exchange holding your coins right now might already be insolvent, using new deposits to cover old withdrawals. You won't know until it's too late.

Understanding What Cold Storage Actually Is

Your crypto never leaves the blockchain. Ever. It doesn't move from the internet into your hardware wallet. Your Bitcoin always lives on the blockchain, distributed across thousands of computers worldwide. You can think of your crypto as a safety deposit box that exists everywhere and nowhere simultaneously. It's secured by mathematical locks on every copy of the blockchain globally. Your hardware wallet doesn't hold the coins. It holds the keys to move them.

When you "send" Bitcoin to your hardware wallet address, you're updating the blockchain to say, "These coins can now be moved only by whoever has this specific private key." The Bitcoin stays on the blockchain; what changes is who can move it.

This is why "not your keys, not your coins" is so profound. Without the keys, you can see Bitcoin on the blockchain, track it, watch it, but you can't move it. You're looking at wealth through bulletproof glass without access.

For the first time in history, you can have absolute mathematical ownership of an asset that no force on earth can take without your keys. Physical gold can be confiscated. Real estate can be seized. Bank accounts can be frozen. But properly secured Bitcoin keys are protected by math that would take all the computers on Earth longer than the universe's age to break.

The Seed Phrase: Your Actual Wealth

When you set up a hardware wallet, it generates a seed phrase, typically 12 or 24 random words. These aren't just a password. They're a mathematical seed that can regenerate every private key your wallet will ever create.

Those 24 words (in wallets using the maximum security standard) can mathematically derive millions of private keys and their corresponding addresses. The number of possible combinations is $2,048^{24}$, or approximately 3.0×10^{79}. There are only about 10^{80} atoms in the observable universe. The chances of someone randomly generating your exact seed phrase are effectively zero.

Anyone with these words can regenerate your entire wallet on any compatible device, anywhere, forever. This is both the power and the danger of seed phrases. They are your wealth in its purest form. But if you lose these words, your crypto is gone forever. No customer service. No password reset. No second chances.

Here's how to protect them properly: Write them on paper with pen, never digitally on any connected device. Never type them into a computer or phone. Never photograph them. Never speak them aloud near any devices with microphones. Store multiple copies in separate secure locations like a home safe, a bank safety deposit box, or with trusted family members in sealed envelopes. Consider metal backup plates that can survive fires and floods, especially for significant holdings.

Some wallets also offer an optional "25th word" passphrase for additional security. This creates a hidden wallet that requires both your seed phrase and this extra passphrase to access. Even if someone finds your 24 words, they can't access funds protected by the additional passphrase.

The fundamental rule: your seed phrase *is* your crypto. Guard it like you would guard gold bars, because, mathematically, it's even more secure than physical gold when properly protected.

Setting Up Your Hardware Wallet

The hardware wallet market evolves rapidly, with new options launching regularly. By the time you are reading this book, there may be excellent wallets that didn't exist when I was writing it. The two most established brands as of this writing are Ledger and Trezor, which have secured billions in value over many years. Other reputable options include Coldcard for Bitcoin maximalists, Keystone for QR-code air-gapped security, and Grid+ Lattice for advanced users. Research current options, but stick with established brands that have been battle-tested through at least one full market cycle.

Whichever wallet you choose, buy directly from the manufacturer's website. Never buy from Amazon, eBay, or third parties, no matter how convenient or cheap they seem. Hardware wallets from third parties could be compromised with malicious firmware, or their seed phrases could already be exposed. That "great deal" on a used wallet could cost you everything.

When your wallet arrives, check for tamper-evident seals and packaging. Different manufacturers use different security measures, so check their website for what to expect. Set it up in a private space without cameras or potential onlookers. The initialization process will generate your seed phrase. This is the most important moment in your crypto journey.

Write down the seed phrase multiple times on paper. Store copies in separate secure locations: home safe, bank safety deposit box, or with a trusted family member in a sealed envelope they won't open. Before moving any significant funds, test the recovery process. Wipe the device completely and restore it from your seed phrase. Generate a receive address, write it down, then wipe and restore again. Verify that the same address appears. This proves your seed phrase works and you've recorded it correctly.

Only after successfully testing recovery should you move meaningful amounts to the wallet. Start with a small test transaction, then gradually move larger amounts once you're confident in the process.

The specific wallet brand matters less than following these security fundamentals. A properly secured budget wallet beats an expensive wallet used carelessly. Your security comes from your practices, not the device itself.

Moving to True Ownership: From Exchange to Cold Storage

Start with a test transaction of $50 to your hardware wallet. Watch it confirm on the blockchain, which will take about an hour for Bitcoin, a few minutes for Ethereum. This small test confirms you have the right address and understand the process before moving larger amounts.

Once successful, move the rest in three to five transactions. This balances safety with fee efficiency: a single mistake won't cost everything, but you're not wasting money on dozens of transfers. As each transaction confirms, you're experiencing something profound: value moving without any bank, government, or company involved. Just you, your keys, and mathematics.

The moment your last Bitcoin leaves the exchange, everything changes. The exchange can't freeze your account, lend your Bitcoin to short sellers, gamble with it like FTX did, or lose it in bankruptcy. Your Bitcoin now exists in its natural state: controlled only by your keys.

This transformation brings capabilities exchange users never have. You can interact directly with DeFi protocols without withdrawal limits or waiting periods. Want to earn 10% on stablecoins instead of 0.05% at your bank? Connect your wallet and start earning immediately. No credit checks, no minimum balances, no branch visits.

You can implement advanced security like multisignature wallets, requiring multiple approvals for large transactions. Think of it like requiring two keys to open a safety deposit box, except you control who holds each key. You could set it up so any purchase over $10,000 requires approval from both you and your spouse, protecting against both hackers and impulsive decisions.

Most importantly, your Bitcoins become unseizable in cold storage. Authorities can freeze exchange accounts with a phone call, but they need physical access to your keys to touch your Bitcoin. This isn't about hiding money; it's about ensuring your savings can't be frozen by a computer error, a mistaken identity, or an overzealous compliance algorithm that locks you out when you need funds most.

The practical benefits are immediate. No more waiting three days for transfers to clear. No more begging for wire transfer approvals. No more panic when banks have "technical difficulties" and you can't access your money. Your crypto is available 24/7/365, anywhere with internet, without asking anyone's permission.

Now, yes, the first night after moving significant crypto to cold storage will test you. You'll find yourself wanting to check your wallet obsessively, worrying about your seed phrase, second-guessing your security setup. This anxiety is normal. We've been trained from childhood to let institutions handle our money. Taking full responsibility feels unnatural, even dangerous.

But after a few weeks, something shifts. Fear transforms into confidence. You realize you're not just capable of being your own bank, you're better at it than actual banks. No banking hours. No arbitrary freezes. No permission needed. I've found that the psychological shift extends beyond crypto. Once you experience true ownership, you question everything else. Your bank account is just the bank's database. Your stocks are your broker's ledger entries. Your 401(k) is locked behind regulations. Bitcoin with your keys might be the only asset you truly own in the absolute sense. No institution between you and your wealth, no one who can dilute or confiscate it.

Eventually you sleep better knowing your crypto is secured by mathematics that would take all computers on Earth longer than the universe's age to crack. You're no longer at the mercy of exchange insolvency or regulatory whims. Your wealth is protected by mathematical laws, which are considerably more reliable than human institutions that fail regularly.

Your Self-Custody Action Plan

Today, if you hold any crypto on an exchange:

1. Order a hardware wallet from the manufacturer directly.
2. When it arrives, set it up, following the instructions exactly.
3. Write down your seed phrase multiple times.
4. Store copies in separate secure locations.
5. Test recovery before moving funds.
6. Move a test amount first.
7. Then move everything else off exchanges in several batches.

Don't overcomplicate it. Don't procrastinate. A basic hardware wallet with your keys is infinitely more secure than the "best" exchange.

The Moment Everything Changes

There's a specific moment when you truly understand self-custody. It's when you realize your crypto exists on thousands of computers worldwide, secured by unbreakable math, and only you have the keys to move it. No government can print more. No bank can lend it without permission. No exchange can gamble with it. No hacker can steal it without physically confronting you.

In that moment, you understand you're not just storing cryptocurrency. You're storing pure economic energy that is yours alone. You're holding an asset that exists outside every traditional system of control.

Crypto gives you the option of financial sovereignty. But it's just an option. If you leave your crypto on an exchange, you're choosing dependence over independence, trust over verification, hope over certainty.

Order your hardware wallet today. Not tomorrow. Not next week. Today. Your future self will thank you when the next exchange falls and your Bitcoin remains safe, exactly where it belongs: on the blockchain, controlled by keys that only you possess. *Your keys. Your coins. Your future.*

9

Ethereum and Smart Contracts: The Internet of Money

The first time I understood what smart contracts can actually do, I was sitting in my apartment at 2 a.m., watching a YouTube video about yield farming. The guy on screen was explaining how his money was earning 80% APY automatically, without any bank, without any company, without any human involvement at all. Just code executing on a blockchain, moving his assets between protocols, harvesting rewards, compounding returns, all while he slept.

My brain broke a little. Not because the returns were high—I'd seen plenty of too-good-to-be-true schemes by then—but because I finally understood: This wasn't a company promising returns. This was code that couldn't do anything except what it was programmed to do. There was no CEO who could run off with funds. No customer service that could freeze accounts. No human decisions at all. Just math executing automatically.

That's when Ethereum clicked for me. Bitcoin had solved digital money. But Ethereum had solved something bigger: programmable money. Money that could think, act, and execute strategies without human intervention. Money that could be its own bank, broker, and financial advisor.

Beyond Digital Gold

If Bitcoin is digital gold, Ethereum is digital everything else. While Bitcoin intentionally stays simple and focuses on being the best money, Ethereum took a different path. Its creator, Vitalik Buterin, was only nineteen when he realized Bitcoin's blockchain could do more than track money. It could run programs.

Not just any programs. Programs that handle money, enforce agreements, and coordinate human activity without any central authority. Programs that, once deployed, run forever exactly as coded. No servers to maintain. No companies to trust. No possibility of censorship or shutdown.

These programs are called smart contracts, though they're not particularly smart and they're not really contracts in the legal sense. They're better understood as unstoppable vending machines. You put in the required inputs (money, data, whatever the contract specifies), and you automatically get the programmed outputs. No negotiation. No interpretation. No possibility of breach.

How Smart Contracts Actually Work

At their core, smart contracts are just if–then statements that execute automatically. If you send 1 ETH to this contract, then it sends you 2,000 USDC. If the price of ETH drops below your liquidation threshold, then your collateral is sold. If thirty days pass since you staked, then you can claim rewards.

The magic isn't in the complexity. It's in the certainty. When you interact with a smart contract, you know exactly what will happen. The code is public, verifiable, and immutable. It can't be bribed, can't discriminate, can't change its mind. It just executes.

Traditional contracts require interpretation, enforcement, and trust that counterparties will fulfill obligations. Smart contracts eliminate all three. The code is the interpretation. The blockchain is the enforcement. Mathematics is the counterparty.

This shift from trusting people to trusting code changes everything. A lending smart contract doesn't care about your credit score, your employment history, or your zip code. It only cares if you have collateral. A trading smart contract doesn't have business hours, holidays, or maintenance windows. It runs 24/7/365 forever.

The Composability Revolution

Here's where Ethereum gets truly revolutionary: smart contracts can interact with other smart contracts. They're like Lego blocks that snap together to create complex financial machines. This *composability* enables innovation at a speed traditional finance can't match.

To understand how radical this is, imagine if your Bank of America account could automatically talk to Charles Schwab, which could instantly communicate with JPMorgan, which could simultaneously interact with Vanguard, all executing complex strategies in perfect coordination without any human involvement. In traditional finance, this would require months of negotiations, legal agreements, API integrations, and millions in development costs. Analogous strategies happen on Ethereum in seconds with a few lines of code.

A single yield-farming contract might interact with dozens of other protocols automatically. It checks lending rates on Aave, Compound, and Euler. Finds the best yield. Moves your funds there. Then it monitors constantly, and when rates change, it withdraws, swaps through Uniswap for optimal routing, and redeploys to the new highest-yielding opportunity. It harvests rewards tokens, sells them at the best price across multiple DEXs, converts proceeds back to your preferred asset, and redeposits to compound your returns. All of this happens 24/7/365 without you lifting a finger.

This is already happening. Right now, billions of dollars are being managed by smart contracts that optimize returns across multiple protocols. They're doing the job of entire hedge funds and their teams of analysts, traders, and portfolio managers, but with perfect execution, no management fees, no coffee breaks, no human error, and complete transparency. You can see every transaction, verify every decision, and audit every line of code.

The speed of this innovation is incomprehensible to traditional finance. When Goldman Sachs wants to integrate with a new financial service, it takes 6–18 months of meetings, contracts, technical integration, and testing. When someone launches a new DeFi protocol on Ethereum, every other protocol can integrate with it immediately. No partnerships needed. No API keys. No business development meetings. No lawyers. No contracts. Just code calling code.

A developer in Nigeria can build a protocol tonight that a protocol in Japan integrates tomorrow, which a user in Brazil benefits from the next day. This permissionless innovation is why DeFi went from zero to hundreds of billions in total value locked in just a few years, while traditional finance takes decades to roll out basic features like instant transfers. This isn't just an improvement on the old system; it's an entirely different paradigm that makes the old system obsolete.

Why Ethereum Dominates Despite Competition

Every cycle, new "Ethereum killers" emerge. Faster! Cheaper! Better! Yet Ethereum maintains overwhelming dominance in DeFi, NFTs, and developer activity. The reason is *network effects*. Every developer building on Ethereum makes it more attractive for the next developer. Every user increases liquidity and opportunity. Every protocol adds to the composability. These effects compound, creating gravity that's nearly impossible to escape.

Developers choose Ethereum not because it's technically superior but because that's where the users, money, and other developers are. Users choose Ethereum because that's where the applications and liquidity are. It's a self-reinforcing cycle that gets stronger over time. Battle-tested security matters, too. Ethereum has secured hundreds of billions for years without critical failure. When you're building financial applications, track record matters more than theoretical performance.

Ethereum isn't some distant future technology. You can use it right now. After securing your assets from chapter 8, your next step is experiencing smart contracts firsthand. Start simple by using a decentralized exchange to swap tokens. Each interaction teaches you how this new system works. Each transaction proves you don't need traditional financial institutions. Sure, the learning curve is a bit steeper: wallets, gas fees, contract interactions are more complex than clicking "buy" on Robinhood. But you're not just learning new software. You're learning the infrastructure of the new financial system.

You might have heard that Ethereum has high gas fees. During the 2021 bull run, fees sometimes hit $50–100 for a single transaction. But that's largely history now. After Ethereum's upgrades and the rise of Layer 2 solutions, mainnet fees typically range from $1–10 for simple transactions, and Layer 2s like Arbitrum, Optimism, and Base offer the same smart contracts with fees under $0.50.

Think of mainnet like Manhattan real estate: premium but not prohibitively expensive anymore. High-value DeFi operations still prefer mainnet's security and liquidity. But just like New York has suburbs connected by bridges and tunnels, Ethereum has Layer 2 solutions making it accessible to everyone.

The future isn't everyone cramming onto mainnet; it's Layer 2s handling daily transactions while mainnet becomes the settlement layer for major operations. We'll explore these in detail in chapter 22. The innovation happening on Ethereum is so valuable that millions of users interact with it daily, and with current fee structures, it's accessible whether you're moving $100 or $100,000.

In Part III, we'll master the markets built on this foundation. In Part IV, you'll discover DeFi strategies that generate real returns, like lending stablecoins for 10% instead of 0.05%, borrowing instantly against collateral without credit checks, providing liquidity, and earning from every trade. These aren't promises. Millions use these services daily with billions flowing through them. But it all starts with understanding that Ethereum isn't just another cryptocurrency. It's the platform on which the entire new economy is being built.

Smart contracts aren't just programs; they're the replacements for every financial intermediary. Not just improvements. *Replacements.* Banks, brokers, exchanges, clearinghouses, all being rebuilt as code that can't be corrupted, can't discriminate, and can't be stopped. The code is law, but more importantly, the code is power. Power to access financial services without permission. Power to verify rather than trust. Power to build wealth through systems that execute exactly as programmed, forever.

10

The Digital Wild West: Protecting Your Wealth in Crypto

Three a.m. My phone buzzes with a Discord notification. Someone's asking for help with their "stuck transaction." They seem desperate, been trying for hours, losing money on a time-sensitive trade. The helpful part of me wants to assist. But something feels off. Their message is too perfect, hitting all the emotional triggers. Urgency. Desperation. Financial loss. They're asking me to check a link to see their transaction details. The URL looks almost right. Almost.

This is how I almost lost everything in my first year. Not to a hack. Not to a smart contract exploit. But to a moment of wanting to help someone who turned out to be a scammer fishing for wallet connections. I was one click away from financial disaster.

Mastering security in crypto isn't optional. Every day, someone loses their entire crypto holdings to a completely preventable attack. Not because the technology failed, but because they made one small mistake. This chapter will help ensure you won't be one of them.

The Threat Landscape You're Entering

The crypto space attracts predators like blood attracts sharks. The combination of irreversible transactions, pseudonymous accounts, and new users unfamiliar with risks creates a perfect hunting ground. But here's what should really concern you: the biggest threat isn't some sophisticated hacker in a dark room. It's your own mistakes.

Most losses come from simple errors. Clicking phishing links that steal wallet access. Sharing seed phrases with fake support. Connecting wallets to malicious sites. Falling for social engineering attacks. Poor password habits leading to exchange account takeovers. Sending funds to wrong addresses. These aren't complex attacks requiring advanced skills to prevent. They're basic traps that catch those who haven't learned to anticipate them.

The beauty and terror of crypto is its finality. When you send Bitcoin to the wrong address, it's gone forever. No customer service can reverse it. No insurance covers it. No government agency can recover it. This irreversibility is what makes crypto powerful, but it's also what makes security absolutely critical. One mistake can cost you everything, and unlike traditional finance, there's no safety net.

The Golden Rules That Will Save You

Never share your seed phrase. This isn't a suggestion or best practice. It's an absolute rule with zero exceptions. MetaMask support doesn't need it. Ledger's validation team doesn't need it. That helpful person in a Discord definitely doesn't need it. No legitimate entity will ever ask for your seed phrase, because they don't need it to help you. Anyone asking for your seed phrase is trying to steal from you. Full stop.

Always verify addresses completely. Check the first four characters, the last four characters, and a few randomly selected ones in the middle. Malware exists that changes copied addresses to attacker addresses, and it's sophisticated enough to generate addresses with similar beginnings and endings. I once caught malware changing my address after copying, and that five-second check saved me $50,000. Make address verification a ritual you never skip, even when sending small amounts. Especially when sending large amounts.

Don't let anyone or anything rush you. The urgency trap catches more victims than any other tactic. Scammers know that rushed decisions are bad decisions. They create artificial time pressure to bypass your critical thinking. Limited-time offers that expire in minutes. Urgent security updates that can't wait. Last chances for whitelists that close imminently. If someone's rushing you, they're likely trying to rob you. Take a breath. Step back. Real opportunities will wait for your due diligence.

Always type the official link or use a verified bookmark. Using official links seems simple, but saves portfolios. Never click links in emails, direct messages, or social media posts. Type URLs manually or use bookmarks you've verified. Fake sites can be pixel-perfect copies with an ersatz URL like mtamask.io instead of metamask.io. One different letter means total loss. The extra seconds spent typing a URL manually could save your entire portfolio. If you're ever unsure about a protocol or platform's legitimate URL, we maintain a vetted list of trusted DeFi platforms and their official links on DeFiBuddy.io. No sign-up required, just a community resource to help you verify you're on the right site before connecting your wallet.

The Most Common Crypto Scams

The fake support scam has destroyed more portfolios than any other attack. You post about a problem in Discord or Telegram, and within seconds, helpful "support team" members message you privately. They're professional, friendly, patient. They have official-looking profiles and speak knowledgeably about your issue. They guide you to a validation site that looks exactly like the real protocol. You enter your seed phrase to verify your wallet. Within minutes, your funds vanish forever.

Real support never initiates contact through DMs. They respond in public channels where others can verify their legitimacy. They solve problems without needing your seed phrase because legitimate support doesn't require seed phrase access. The moment someone DMs you offering help, your defenses should activate. Thank them politely and ask them to help you in the public channel.

Phishing sites have become so sophisticated that even experienced users fall for them. You search for a protocol, click what looks like the right result, connect your wallet, and approve what seems like a normal transaction. But instead of the intended interaction, you've just given unlimited approval for attackers to drain your wallet. These sites often appear as ads above real search results, use domains that differ by one character, and replicate the legitimate site's design perfectly.

The solution isn't just vigilance but systematic precaution. Bookmark legitimate sites after carefully verifying them. Use the official links from DeFiBuddy.io or the protocol's verified Twitter. When in doubt, cross-reference URLs across multiple sources. That extra minute of verification could save years of accumulated wealth.

Rug pulls represent the most brazen theft method in crypto. A new token launches with massive marketing, celebrity endorsements, and promises of revolution. The Telegram group has thousands of members generating hype. The website looks professional. The white paper promises to solve every problem in crypto. You invest $5,000 in what seems like the opportunity of a lifetime.

Within hours or days, the developers pull all liquidity from trading pools. The website disappears. The Telegram goes silent. Your tokens become untradeable and worthless. The entire project was orchestrated theft from the beginning. The community, the excitement, the technology, all of it was theater designed to separate you from your money.

The Human Element of Security

The most sophisticated security measures fail when humans make predictable mistakes. You are the weakest link in your security chain, but acknowledging this makes you stronger, not weaker.

If you have more than $10,000 in crypto, you need a hardware wallet. We covered this in chapter 8, but it bears repeating: hardware wallets transform security from a hope that hackers won't target you to mathematical certainty that they can't succeed even if they do. Every day your crypto sits in a hot wallet connected to the internet is a day you're gambling with your wealth.

Two-factor authentication using an authenticator app (never SMS, which can be hijacked) transforms your security. Most "hacks" are just attackers getting passwords and logging in. With 2FA, knowing your password isn't enough. They need physical access to your device, making remote attacks impossible.

Social engineering works because attackers understand psychology better than their victims understand security. They create scenarios that trigger emotions: fear of missing out, panic about losing funds, desire to help others, excitement about opportunities. Each emotion becomes an attack vector. The defense isn't to become emotionless but to recognize when your emotions are being manipulated.

Building automatic security habits protects you when attention lapses. Always hover over links before clicking. Always verify addresses completely. Never rush transactions. These habits protect you when you're tired, distracted, or emotional, which is when most mistakes happen.

When Things Go Wrong

If you click a phishing link, seconds matter. Immediately disconnect from the internet. Transfer funds to a new wallet using a different device. Revoke all approvals on the compromised wallet. Never use that wallet again, even if it seems fine. Attackers often wait for you to deposit more funds before striking.

The psychological aftermath often hurts more than financial losses. Victims feel stupid, ashamed, angry at themselves. But these incidents happen to smart, careful people every day. The technology is new, the attacks are sophisticated, and humans make mistakes. Learn from the incident, improve your security, help others avoid the same fate, but don't let one mistake define your crypto journey.

The Security Mindset

Surviving and thriving in crypto requires calibrated paranoia. Not the kind that prevents participation, but the kind that ensures safe participation. Assume every DM is a scam until proven otherwise. Assume every new protocol might rug until proven legitimate. Assume every link might be phishing until verified safe.

But security shouldn't become paralysis. The goal isn't avoiding all risk but managing it intelligently. Use security measures appropriate to your holdings. Someone with $1,000 in crypto needs different security than someone with

$1,000,000. Find your balance between protection and participation. New attack vectors emerge constantly. Yesterday's security measures become today's vulnerabilities. Staying secure means staying educated, staying vigilant, and staying humble about the risks. The moment you think you're too smart to fall for scams is the moment you become vulnerable to them.

Remember what you're protecting: not just tokens or coins, but your time, effort, dreams, and future converted into digital form. Every security measure you implement is insurance against catastrophic loss. The inconvenience of 2FA is nothing compared to the upheaval of losing everything. The cost of a hardware wallet is nothing compared to the cost of losing your wealth. The effort required for good operational security is nothing compared to years or decades of extra work you'll face if you lose everything to a scam.

The Wild West analogy everyone uses for crypto is apt but incomplete. The Wild West eventually got sheriffs, laws, and safety. Crypto might get there, too, but we're not there yet. Right now, you're your own sheriff, your own security, your own last line of defense. Think of it as the price of sovereignty. And once you understand that, once you implement proper security, you realize it's a small price to pay for true financial freedom.

Part III:

Market Mastery

11

Market Cycles and Psychology:
How the Crowd Creates Opportunities

Maybe you can relate: I was watching my portfolio evaporate in real time. Every refresh brought more red. Bitcoin down 15%. Ethereum down 22%. My altcoins? Don't even ask. In a panic, I sold everything at the absolute bottom, locking in a $10,000 loss. Three months later, the market rebounded 40%. Of course it did. So I FOMOed back in, buying higher than I sold. Then it dropped again. I sold again. Lower this time. The market bounced. I bought back. Higher. Again.

I was always two steps behind, always buying what just pumped and selling what just dumped. Every decision was emotional. Every trade was reactive. I had no idea that markets move in predictable patterns. I didn't understand that Bitcoin leads, then Ethereum follows, then large caps pump, then altseason arrives. I was playing a game without knowing the rules, hemorrhaging money with every move.

It took me a full cycle to finally understand the rhythm of crypto. Once I saw it, everything changed. When everyone's euphoric, I take profits. When everyone's terrified, I accumulate. When Bitcoin starts its run, I'm already positioned in Ethereum for what comes next. No longer two steps behind, but positioned ahead, ready to lock in gains instead of chasing ghosts.

The Rhythm That Governs Everything

Crypto markets look chaotic, but they follow a rhythm as predictable as seasons. Once you see this pattern, you can't unsee it. More importantly, once you understand it, you stop being its victim and start being its beneficiary.

The master pattern is Bitcoin's four-year halving cycle. Every four years, the amount of new Bitcoin created gets cut in half. This creates a supply shock that ripples through the entire crypto ecosystem. It's not theory or speculation. It's mathematical certainty written into Bitcoin's code.

Here's how it has played out every single time. The halving occurs, reducing new supply. For months, nothing seems to happen. Price stays flat or barely moves. People get bored and declare the halving priced in. Then, gradually, the supply shortage builds pressure. Price starts climbing. Media notices. Retail investors return. FOMO kicks in. Parabolic rise. Unsustainable euphoria. A reset. Depression. Accumulation by smart money. Next halving. Repeat.

The 2012 halving led to 2013's rise from $12 to $1,200. The 2016 halving led to 2017's rise from $650 to $20,000. The 2020 halving led to 2021's rise from $8,000 to $69,000. The pattern isn't perfect, but it's consistent enough to build wealth if you position correctly.

But there's more. Within this four-year macro cycle lives a micro pattern that most people miss: the flow of capital from Bitcoin to Ethereum to large caps to altseason. Understanding this flow is the difference between catching small waves and riding a tsunami.

The Capital Flow Pattern

After watching this pattern play out multiple times and helping thousands navigate it through the Underdog Investor Group and the communities we've built, I can now see it coming like clockwork.

Phase 1: Bitcoin leads. Every bull cycle starts with Bitcoin. Always. Without exception. New money enters crypto through Bitcoin because it's the king, the original, the one everyone knows. Institutional investors buy Bitcoin first. Companies add Bitcoin to balance sheets. ETFs launch for Bitcoin. The media talks about Bitcoin.

During this phase, Bitcoin dominance rises (that's Bitcoin's percentage of total crypto market cap). When this metric climbs from 40% to 60% or higher, it's telling you money is flooding into Bitcoin faster than anywhere else. Your altcoins might be up 20% in dollars, but if Bitcoin is up 50%, you're actually losing ground in BTC terms.

This creates a psychological torture chamber for altcoin holders. They watch their bags bleed against Bitcoin day after day. The Bitcoin maximalists become insufferable, posting "told you so" memes. Eventually, altcoin holders capitulate, selling their positions to rotate back into Bitcoin—usually at exactly the wrong time, right before the rotation begins.

The smart money operates differently. While everyone's chasing Bitcoin's pump, they're quietly accumulating Ethereum at suppressed ratios, knowing what comes next. This is when you should already be positioned: not chasing Bitcoin after it's moved, but holding it from bear market accumulation while preparing for the next phase.

Phase 2: Ethereum awakens. As Bitcoin hits new highs and starts feeling expensive to new entrants, capital begins flowing to Ethereum. The narrative shifts dramatically. Suddenly everyone remembers that "Bitcoin is just digital gold, but Ethereum is the world's computer." The flippening narrative returns.

Watch the ETH/BTC ratio during this phase. It starts climbing relentlessly. Where 0.03 ETH per BTC seemed normal, suddenly it's 0.05, then 0.07. Ethereum begins outperforming Bitcoin consistently, sometimes dramatically. This phase overlaps with Bitcoin's continued rise. Money isn't leaving Bitcoin yet; new money is flowing to both. But Ethereum starts capturing the lion's share of fresh capital. DeFi protocols on Ethereum explode. Gas fees spike from activity. Everyone remembers why Ethereum matters.

Phase 3: Large-cap mania. Now the market gets interesting. Bitcoin and Ethereum have both made massive moves. New entrants missed the boat on both and are desperately seeking "the next Bitcoin" or "the next Ethereum." Capital flows aggressively to large-cap altcoins. Examples as of this writing are Solana, Cardano, Sui, XRP, or whatever's in the top 20.

The narratives are predictably uniform. Every large cap is an "Ethereum killer" with "superior technology" that's "faster and cheaper." Whether these claims are true becomes irrelevant. Capital is flowing down the risk curve, seeking higher multiples. These large caps start pulling explosive moves—2x, 3x, 5x—while Bitcoin consolidates sideways.

Crypto Twitter transforms into tribal warfare. Every large cap develops a rabid community. Solana maxis battle Ethereum maxis. The Cardano army attacks everyone. Avalanche supporters claim inevitable dominance. Charts showing their coin "flipping" Ethereum get thousands of retweets. The intensity of these arguments is your signal: when tribalism reaches fever pitch, large caps are overheated.

Phase 4: Peak altseason insanity. This is the final phase before everything resets, and it's absolutely spectacular to witness. Large caps have gone parabolic, and now capital flows to literally everything. Small caps pump 10x in a week. Memecoins do 100x in days. Complete garbage with no website, no team, no white paper, sometimes just a name and logo, pumps 50x because someone on TikTok mentioned it.

The mainstream invasion begins. Your hairdresser is shilling you a coin they can't pronounce. Your Uber driver just quit to day-trade full time. Your grandmother asks if she should buy Dogecoin. Local news runs daily crypto segments. Celebrities launch tokens. Athletes change their Twitter names to include ".eth". LinkedIn becomes insufferable with everyone suddenly a "blockchain expert."

Twitter transforms into pure mania. Nothing but rocket emojis, "LFG!", "WAGMI", and price predictions that would make Bitcoin worth more than all assets on Earth combined. Technical analysis charts showing parabolic curves to infinity. Everyone posting screenshots of their 100x gains. The few voices urging caution get drowned out by euphoria.

During peak altseason, fundamentals become completely irrelevant. Good projects pump. Terrible projects pump harder. Memes outperform infrastructure. Dog coins outperform revolutionary technology. A token called "Useless" goes up 1000%. The market has completely detached from reality, and it feels like it will last forever.

This is precisely when you should be aggressively taking profits, paying off debt, closing leveraged positions, and converting a significant portion to stablecoins. Because what comes next is brutal for anyone leveraged, overexposed, or convinced that "this time is different."

Phase 5: The reset. Then it happens. Sometimes it's triggered by a specific event like an exchange hack, regulatory crackdown, or macro shock. Sometimes it's just exhaustion, like a party that's gone on too long. But the music stops. Bitcoin drops 30% in a week. Altcoins crater 50% to 70%. Leveraged traders get liquidated in cascading waterfalls of forced selling.

The psychological whiplash is extreme. The same people who were posting Lambo pics last week are now debating whether crypto is all a scam. Projects that were "revolutionary" suddenly look questionable. Teams go silent. Telegram groups that had thousands of messages daily become ghost towns.

The media, which was breathlessly covering crypto's rise, now celebrates its demise with barely concealed glee. "Bitcoin Crashes" becomes the favorite headline. Regulators suddenly get aggressive, proposing restrictions they'd never dare during bull markets. Exchanges start having mysterious "technical issues" during the most volatile moments.

But these resets aren't disasters, they're opportunities. They clear out excess leverage, reset valuations to reasonable levels, and shake out weak hands who were only here for quick gains. Those who took profits during euphoria now have dry powder to deploy at 70% discounts. The reset creates the foundation for the next cycle.

The Psychology that Drives It All

Remember that markets are made of humans, and humans are emotional creatures. The cycle isn't driven by technology adoption or fundamental value. It's driven by the predictable oscillation between fear and greed, playing out in the minds of millions of individuals simultaneously.

Every candlestick on the chart represents human emotion crystallized into price action. That massive red candle isn't just a price plummeting. It's thousands of people panicking, capitulating, giving up hope, swearing off crypto forever. And that green candle isn't just a price rising. It's FOMO incarnate, dreams of wealth, the fear of missing out overwhelming rational thought.

I used to be pure emotion. Every pump triggered dopamine hits and fantasies of early retirement. Every dump triggered cortisol spikes and existential dread. I was a puppet dancing to the market's strings, always reacting, never anticipating. My mood swings directly correlated with my portfolio performance.

The transformation came when I realized my emotions weren't unique; they were the market's emotions as well. When I felt maximum FOMO, so did millions of others. When I felt crushing despair, a collective despair was creating the bottom. My emotions became a contrarian indicator. That churning anxiety when Bitcoin drops 20%? That's the exact feeling that creates capitulation candles and generates opportunity.

Your brain evolved to survive on the savanna, not to navigate financial markets. When everyone runs from danger, your instinct says run too. This kept your ancestors alive, but in markets it destroys wealth. The comfort of consensus (buying when everyone's buying, selling when everyone's selling) feels safe but guarantees mediocre results.

Your Cycle Action Plan

Understanding cycles intellectually is worthless without an action plan. Right now, as you read this, we're somewhere in this cycle. Your job is to identify where and position accordingly.

Start by analyzing objective metrics. What's Bitcoin dominance doing? If it's rising from cycle lows, we're likely in phase 1. Check the ETH/BTC ratio. Is it near cycle lows or starting to climb? Monitor large cap performance against Bitcoin and Ethereum. Track social sentiment through the CNN Business Fear & Greed Index. Count the crypto segments on mainstream media. Bookmark DefiBuddy.io and use it often to research, analyze, and assess markets, assets, and opportunities.

Once you've identified the phase, position for what's coming next, not what's happening now. If Bitcoin is leading, accumulate Ethereum at suppressed ratios. If Ethereum is outperforming, research quality large caps before they pump. If large caps are going parabolic, prepare for altseason but also start taking profits.

Create your rotation strategy now, while you're rational. Write it down. Maybe it's moving 30% from Bitcoin to Ethereum when the ratio hits certain levels. Maybe it's taking 25% profits every time a position doubles. Maybe it's converting 10% to stablecoins every month during euphoria phases. We'll explore specific profit-taking strategies in chapter 16, but for now, create a rough draft.

Most importantly, respect the reset. When it comes, and it always comes, don't panic-sell the bottom. Have dry powder ready. View 70% discounts as opportunities, not disasters. The same people calling for $1 million Bitcoin during euphoria will call for $10,000 Bitcoin during despair. Both are wrong. The truth is always somewhere between the extremes.

Remember: Amateurs react to what just happened. Professionals position for what will happen next. Tourists arrive during altseason and leave during bear markets. Influencers multiply during bulls and vanish during bears. But those who truly understand cycles, including you now, accumulate during bloodbaths and distribute during euphoria.

The cycle will continue whether you understand it or not. Bitcoin will lead, Ethereum will follow, large caps will pump, altseason will arrive, and then everything will reset. The only question is whether you'll be positioned ahead of the moves or forever chasing yesterday's pumps.

12

The HODL Philosophy:
Getting Rich by Doing Nothing

Last chapter, we explored the predictable cycles that govern crypto markets. Bitcoin leads, Ethereum follows, large caps pump, then altseason arrives. The pattern is clear, the rhythm predictable. Armed with this knowledge, you might think the optimal strategy is to time these transitions perfectly, like selling 100% of your Bitcoin at its peak to buy Ethereum, rotating to large caps at just the right moment, then riding altseason to maximum gains.

Here's the problem: trying to time these cycles perfectly will likely make you poorer, not richer. The vast majority of people who attempt to trade these transitions end up with less Bitcoin than if they'd simply held. They sell too early, buy back too late, miss entire moves while waiting for dips that never come. The tax implications alone can destroy years of gains.

This chapter explores a counterintuitive truth: in a market where cycles are predictable but timing is impossible, the highest-probability path to wealth is often doing absolutely nothing. HODLing consistently outperforms clever trading for one simple reason: it removes the possibility of making the worst mistake in crypto, selling an exponentially appreciating asset too early.

The Drunken Typo That Became a Philosophy for Life

December 18, 2013. Bitcoin had just crashed from $1,163 to $522 in a matter of days. If you understood cycles, you might have recognized this as a typical correction after a parabolic rise. But emotions were high, and the forums were in chaos. People were declaring crypto dead, calling it a scam, posting about devastating losses.

Then, at 10:03 a.m., a user named GameKyuubi posted something that would become legendary: "I AM HODLING."

He was drunk. He meant to type "holding." But in his rambling, intoxicated post about being a terrible trader and knowing he'd just lose more money if he sold, he accidentally created a meme-worthy term for the most powerful investment philosophy in history.

That drunken typo became more than a meme. It became the strategy that separated winners from losers, wealth builders from wealth destroyers. And it perfectly captures a truth that Warren Buffett has been preaching for decades: "Our favorite holding period is forever."

The Math That Should Change Your Approach

Let me show you the mathematical reality of HODLing through the worst crashes, because numbers don't lie, even when our emotions do.

March 2020. COVID hit. Markets imploded. Bitcoin crashed from around $10,000 to $3,800 in a matter of weeks. A 62% loss—the kind of drop that makes your stomach turn, that triggers every survival instinct to sell and salvage what's left.

Anyone who sold at $3,800 locked in that 62% loss forever. They crystallized their pain into permanent reality. They took what traders call a "realized loss" and made it irreversible. But here's what happened to those who HODLed: eighteen months later, Bitcoin hit $69,000. That's not just a recovery. That's an 18x return from the bottom. Even from the pre-crash price of $10,000, holders saw nearly a 7x return.

The seller at $3,800 lost 62% permanently. The HODLer gained 690%. This isn't an isolated incident. This is the pattern that repeats every single cycle.

As Paul Tudor Jones put it when he allocated to Bitcoin: "The best profit-maximizing strategy is to own the fastest horse." The HODLers aren't trying to time the race. They're just making sure they own the horse.

The Four-Year Reality That Changes Everything

Here's the fact that should be carved in stone above every crypto investor's desk: Bitcoin has never had a negative return over any four-year period. Ever. Pick any date in Bitcoin's history. Any date. If you bought that day, then held for four years, you made money. It doesn't matter if you bought at the absolute peak. It doesn't matter if you had the worst timing imaginable. Four years later, you were in profit.

Bought at the 2013 peak of $1,163? By 2017, you were up 1,600%. Bought at the 2017 peak of $20,000? By 2021, you were up 245%. Bought at the 2021 peak of $69,000? We're already seeing recovery with Bitcoin above $100,000.

This isn't luck or hope. It's mathematics. Bitcoin's fixed supply combined with growing adoption creates what we call a ratchet effect. Each cycle brings new holders who don't sell. Each crash has a higher floor than the last. Each peak reaches further into price discovery.

And here's what's different now: institutional money doesn't gamble. When MicroStrategy puts billions into Bitcoin, they're not day trading. When Tesla adds Bitcoin to their balance sheet, they're not panic-selling on red days. When insurance companies and pension funds allocate to Bitcoin, they're thinking in decades, not days.

The launch of Bitcoin ETFs changed everything. In January 2024, the SEC finally approved spot Bitcoin ETFs, and within months, these funds absorbed billions in institutional capital. BlackRock's Bitcoin ETF became one of the fastest-growing ETFs in history. These weren't retail traders with weak hands. These were institutional allocators with investment committees, risk management frameworks, and holding periods measured in years or decades.

Your grandmother's pension fund can now own Bitcoin. Corporate treasuries can allocate without dealing with custody. Sovereign wealth funds can gain exposure through regulated products. This isn't speculative money that runs at the first sign of trouble. This is institutional capital that rebalances quarterly at most. As Michael Saylor says: "Bitcoin is a bank in cyberspace, run by incorruptible software." Institutions understand this. They're not buying the volatility; they're buying the certainty of the protocol.

Each wave of institutional adoption creates a higher floor. The 2017 cycle was retail FOMO. The 2021 cycle brought corporate treasuries. The 2024 cycle brought ETFs and institutional allocation. The next cycle? Central banks are already discussing Bitcoin reserves.

The difference between temporary loss and permanent wealth is just time and conviction. Every Bitcoin you HODL today is a vote for your future prosperity.

Why Your Brain Is Your Worst Enemy

The human brain evolved to keep you alive on the African savanna 100,000 years ago. When you see danger, like a price dropping, your amygdala screams to run. When you see others fleeing through panic selling, your herd instinct says to follow. These instincts kept your ancestors from being eaten by lions. But in markets, these same instincts guarantee you'll buy high and sell low.

When Bitcoin crashes 25%, your brain literally cannot tell the difference between numbers on a screen changing and a physical threat to your life. The stress hormones flooding your system are identical. The fight-or-flight response is the same. Your body is preparing you to survive a lion attack, not a market correction.

This is why HODLing feels impossible during crashes. You're not fighting the market. You're fighting millions of years of evolution. Your own biology is working against you. The people who get wealthy in crypto aren't smarter or better at predicting prices. They're just better at doing nothing when their brain screams at them to do something. As Buffett puts it, "The stock market is designed to transfer money from the active to the patient."

In the communities I've built, we have a saying: "Do nothing." It sounds simple, but it's profound. The best move during emotional markets is often to not click any buttons. Volatility triggers fear and FOMO that lead most investors to make their worst decisions. By zooming out, focusing on your time horizon, and following predefined rules instead of emotions, you turn patience into an edge.

Plus, if you're building a DeFi portfolio as we'll explore in Part IV, you literally profit from that volatility in the form of higher trading fees. While others panic, your liquidity pools are earning.

The Million-Dollar Bitcoin Thesis

I personally don't see a future where Bitcoin isn't worth a million dollars per coin. Not because I'm an optimist, but because I understand the fundamentals.

There will only ever be 21 million Bitcoin. But there are 59 million millionaires in the world today. If each one wanted just one Bitcoin, they couldn't have it. There aren't enough. The math is that simple.

Ray Dalio, who was once a Bitcoin skeptic, now says: "Bitcoin has established itself as something like a digital gold." When the founder of the world's largest hedge fund compares Bitcoin to gold, pay attention. Gold has a $25 trillion market cap. Bitcoin at $2 trillion is still early.

Factor in corporations adding Bitcoin to balance sheets. Countries adding Bitcoin to reserves. Billions of people using it as savings. A generation growing up with crypto as normal. The demand trajectory is clear while supply is fixed.

A million-dollar Bitcoin isn't a crazy prediction. It's conservative. That's only a 10x from current prices. Bitcoin has done 10x moves in single years before. Over a decade? It's not just possible, it's probable.

This is why it's always a good time to buy Bitcoin, regardless of what markets are doing. If you're thinking in terms of million-dollar Bitcoin, does it really matter if you buy at $100,000, $70,000, or $50,000? That's like debating whether to buy Manhattan real estate at $100 or $75 per square foot in 1970. The person who bought at either price is wealthy today.

The Psychology of Diamond Hands

In my opinion, HODLing isn't passive. It's the most active form of investing because you're constantly fighting your own psychology. Building diamond hands requires several mental shifts.

First, never invest more than you can afford to lose. If a 40% drop would ruin your life, your position is too large. Size accordingly. This removes the pressure that forces poor decisions.

Think in Bitcoin, not dollars. You don't own "$70,000 of Bitcoin." You own 1 Bitcoin. The dollar price is irrelevant if you're not selling. This mental shift changes everything about how you perceive volatility.

Remember that every Bitcoin you HODL is removed from the market. It's not being sold for fiat. It's not available to short sellers. It's not sitting on an exchange waiting to be dumped. HODLers are slowly draining Bitcoin from the available supply. Each cycle, more Bitcoin moves from weak hands to diamond hands. From traders to holders. From speculators to believers. Long-term holders now control over 70% of Bitcoin supply. This number only goes up over time. We're watching a supply squeeze in slow motion.

The beautiful part is you can earn yield on your Bitcoin through DeFi while HODLing. You can borrow against it instead of selling. You can generate income from it without giving up ownership. This turns HODLing from a waiting game into a wealth-building system. We'll explore these strategies in depth in Part IV.

With all that said, the path to diamond hands follows predictable stages. At first, you'll check prices every hour and feel every 10% move in your soul. Then you'll check daily and start seeing patterns instead of panic. Eventually, you'll check weekly and feel confident during crashes. Finally, you'll check monthly and actually get excited about buying opportunities during bear markets. That's when you know you've arrived.

The real question isn't whether Bitcoin will reach a million dollars. Given the fundamentals, that's essentially inevitable. The question is whether you'll still be HODLing when it does. Time is your friend. Time in the market beats timing the market.

GameKyuubi's drunken typo became the modern-day symbol for a philosophy because it captured a timeless truth: the distance between poverty and wealth is measured in patience, not intelligence. Luckily, the formula is simple. Buy Bitcoin and other strong blue-chip assets. HODL through volatility. Generate yield while waiting. Let time do the heavy lifting. The only thing standing between you and wealth is your own fear, impatience, and greed.

13

Why Chaos Creates Wealth: Profiting in Uncertainty

Volatility is the price of admission to life-changing returns, yet most people treat it like a disease to be cured. They want crypto's 1000x gains without the 80% drawdowns. They want DeFi yields without price swings. They want the reward without the ride. This fundamental misunderstanding of volatility's role keeps them poor, while those who embrace it build wealth.

Here's the truth traditional finance doesn't want you to understand: volatility isn't risk; it's opportunity compressed into time. Every wild swing that sends tourists running creates income for those positioned correctly. Every crash that triggers panic selling enables systematic accumulation. Every pump that creates euphoria generates fees for liquidity providers. Volatility isn't the enemy of wealth building; it's the engine that powers it.

The same volatility that destroys emotional traders enriches systematic investors. While others stare at charts and pray for stability, we're earning fees from their panic trades. While they're losing sleep over 30% drops, we're providing the liquidity that enables their exit. We don't fear volatility; we farm it.

The Mathematics That Should Excite You

Volatility and returns are mathematically inseparable in free markets. This isn't opinion; it's observable fact across every asset class in history. Assets with higher volatility deliver higher returns over time, not despite the volatility but because of it. The volatility is the mechanism through which returns are generated.

Bitcoin's volatility is roughly four times higher than that of the S&P 500. Its returns are also roughly ten times higher over the past decade. Ethereum's volatility exceeds Bitcoin's by 50%. Its returns have exceeded Bitcoin's by 300% since genesis. The pattern is consistent: more volatility equals more opportunity for those who can withstand it. Talk about placing an asymmetric bet!

Traditional finance uses volatility as a proxy for risk, which makes sense when your goal is preserving the wealth you've already built. But when your goal is building wealth, volatility becomes your ally. A 50% drawdown in an asset trending up long-term isn't a disaster; it's a discount sale. A 200% pump isn't unsustainable; it's a chance to take profits and reload. The volatility enables both the accumulation and the distribution that create long-term wealth.

Consider the mathematical reality of crypto's volatility. Bitcoin has experienced five drawdowns exceeding 70%. After each one, it reached new all-time highs. Ethereum has crashed 90% or more multiple times. Each crash preceded even higher peaks. The volatility wasn't incidental to the gains; it was instrumental to them. Weak hands transferred their holdings to strong hands at discounted prices, concentrating ownership among those who understood the long-term trajectory.

Markets require volatility to function efficiently. Price discovery happens through oscillation, not stability. Value gets determined through the constant push and pull of buyers and sellers disagreeing on price. Remove volatility, and you remove the mechanism through which markets find fair value. A flat line on a chart isn't stability; it's death.

How DeFi Transforms Volatility Into Income

Traditional investors see volatility as something to endure. DeFi investors see it as something to harvest. Every price movement in either direction generates trading volume. Every trade generates fees. Every fee gets distributed to liquidity providers. The more volatile the market, the more income we generate.

When ETH swings 20% in a day, trading volume explodes. Traders trying to catch the move. Arbitrageurs balancing prices across exchanges. Liquidators closing underwater positions. Each transaction pays fees to the liquidity pools that enable the trades. As a liquidity provider, you're not betting on direction; you're profiting from movement itself.

The beauty of this model is its indifference to price direction. Market pumping? Traders buy ETH from your pool, paying fees. Market dumping? Traders sell ETH to your pool, paying fees. Sideways chop? Traders oscillate between buying and selling, paying fees on every reversal. The volatility that destroys directional traders enriches neutral liquidity providers.

During the May 2021 crash, when ETH dropped from $4,300 to $1,700 in days, Uniswap processed over $10 billion in volume. Liquidity providers earned millions in fees from panic sellers and bottom buyers. The same volatility that wiped out leveraged traders created the highest fee generation in DeFi history.

We'll dive deep into liquidity provision strategies in chapter 18, but understand this: volatility isn't the problem; it's the solution. The temporary impermanent loss from price divergence gets compensated by permanent gains from fee accumulation. Without volatility, there's no trading. Without trading, there are no fees. Volatility literally creates the opportunity.

The Psychology That Separates Winners From Losers

As we explored in chapters 11 and 12, our brains interpret volatility as danger, and winners reprogram this response through understanding. The key addition to your understanding in this chapter is that volatility is a filter mechanism. Every crash shakes out weak hands, concentrating ownership among those with conviction. Every pump attracts new participants who become future sellers. This constant filtering ensures that long-term holders accumulate larger positions over time. The volatility that scares others away is literally the mechanism through which you build wealth.

Paradoxically, the most dangerous markets are the stable ones. Low volatility breeds complacency, excessive leverage, and systematic risk that explodes suddenly. The 2008 financial crisis followed a period called "The Great Moderation," when volatility was historically low. The calm preceded the storm.

In crypto, periods of low volatility are accumulation phases before explosive moves. When Bitcoin spends months in a tight range, that isn't stability; it's a coiled spring building energy. When volatility compresses, it's not disappearing; it's loading up for expansion. These quiet periods are when smart money positions for the inevitable volatility return.

Low volatility also means low opportunity. If Bitcoin moved only 1% daily like forex pairs, the returns would match forex returns. The 100x gains come from 100x volatility. Wishing for stability while wanting exponential returns is requesting the impossible. You can have stable purchasing power preservation or volatile wealth multiplication, not both.

The opportunity cost of avoiding volatility is enormous. Every investor waiting for crypto to "become stable" before entering is waiting for returns to normalize to traditional market levels. By the time volatility decreases to comfortable levels, the exponential gains are behind us. The volatility isn't a bug to be fixed; it's the feature that creates opportunity.

Volatility as Your Wealth-Building Tool

Sophisticated investors treat volatility as an accumulation mechanism rather than something to avoid. Every significant drop is an opportunity to acquire assets at discounted prices. Every pump is a chance to take profits and reload for the next cycle. Volatility enables this systematic accumulation and distribution that builds long-term wealth.

If you're HODLing instead of trading, then dollar-cost averaging works precisely because of volatility. Buying the same dollar amount regularly means acquiring more units when prices are low, fewer when high. Over time, your average cost basis becomes lower than the average price. The greater the swings, the better DCA performs relative to lump sum investing. Volatility literally makes your strategy more profitable.

The accumulation mindset transforms volatility from enemy to ally. Instead of fearing the next 50% crash, you prepare for it with dry powder. Instead of celebrating unsustainable pumps, you take profits and sit tight. Volatility becomes the mechanism through which you build positions larger than you could otherwise afford.

Think about this: every Bitcoin you buy during a 50% crash is essentially half price. Every profit you take during a parabolic rise comes from selling at premium prices. The volatility creates these opportunities. Without it, you'd be stuck buying and selling at fair value forever, generating market returns instead of life-changing wealth.

The Future of Volatility (And Your Opportunity Window)

Volatility in crypto will decrease over time, but we're still years away from stability. As market caps grow, the same dollar flows create smaller-percentage moves. As institutions enter, their steady accumulation dampens wild swings. As derivatives markets mature, hedging mechanisms smooth price discovery.

But this volatility decrease is gradual, not sudden. Bitcoin's volatility today is lower than five years ago but still multiples higher than that of traditional assets. Ethereum's volatility exceeds Bitcoin's. Smaller-cap assets remain wildly volatile. The opportunity to profit from volatility in Bitcoin will exist for years, possibly decades.

Understanding this trajectory is crucial for timing your wealth building. The highest volatility and returns are behind us in Bitcoin, still available in Ethereum, and abundant in smaller projects. As an asset matures, its volatility naturally decreases. This progression from extreme volatility to relative stability is predictable and exploitable.

The smart approach is to capture the volatility premium while it exists. Generate fees from volatile trading pairs now, because they won't be volatile forever. Accumulate during drawdowns now, because they're becoming shallower. Take profits during pumps now, because they're becoming smaller. The window for volatility-based strategies is still open, but it's closing gradually.

Embracing Chaos as Opportunity

Volatility isn't something to overcome in crypto; it's something to understand, embrace, and use. Every swing that terrifies traditional investors enriches those who understand volatility's role in wealth creation. Ultimately, it'll be your relationship with volatility that determines your success in crypto. Fear volatility, and you'll buy tops and sell bottoms. Understand it, and you'll accumulate systematically. Embrace it, and you'll generate income from others' emotional reactions. Master it, and you'll build wealth while others build anxiety.

Every wild swing is a wealth transfer from the emotional to the systematic, from traders to investors, from tourists to natives. Position yourself on the receiving end of these transfers. Provide liquidity during chaos. Accumulate during despair. Lock in profits during euphoria. Let volatility work for you rather than against you.

Remember: the same volatility that makes crypto unsuitable for conservative investors makes it perfect for wealth builders. You can't have exponential gains without exponential volatility. They're two sides of the same coin. Embrace both or receive neither.

14

Due Diligence Secrets:
How to Invest With Confidence,
Not Guesswork

Pull up CoinGecko or CoinMarketCap right now and scroll past the top 100. Keep scrolling. Past 500. Past 1,000. Keep going to page 50, 60, 70. What you're looking at is a graveyard. Twenty thousand–plus projects, and 95% of them are either dead or dying or they were scams from day one. Each had a website, a white paper, a Telegram group full of believers. People invested their life savings believing they'd found the next Bitcoin. Now they're digital tombstones, monuments to hype without substance.

I've contributed to that graveyard myself. In 2021, I found a project that seemed perfect. Revolutionary technology, celebrity endorsements, massive community, beautiful website, professional marketing. The CEO did interviews on major podcasts. They had partnerships with "major corporations" that were never actually named. The Telegram had 50,000 members all screaming, "To the moon!"

I put in $20,000 from my business profits. Six months later, my investment was worth $300. Not a typo. Three hundred dollars.

Meanwhile, that same year, I passed on a project with an ugly website, an anonymous team, and maybe 500 people in their Discord. No marketing budget. No celebrity shills. Just developers building something that actually worked. That $5,000 investment I didn't make would have turned into $240,000 over the next twelve months.

The difference? One project had everything except quality. The other had quality and nothing else. After losing money on dozens of garbage projects and making money on a handful of quality ones, I developed a framework for separating substance from hype. This chapter gives you that framework, refined through years of expensive education in the markets.

Why 95% of Projects Are Destined to Die

The crypto graveyard exists because creating a token is trivially easy. You can launch an ERC-20 token in fifteen minutes for less than $100. Create a website with AI in an hour. Write a white paper full of buzzwords in an afternoon. Suddenly you have a "project" that looks legitimate to newcomers.

But looking legitimate and being legitimate are completely different things. Most projects are solutions looking for problems. They start with "Let's make a token" instead of "Let's solve this specific issue." The token exists to make founders rich, not to enable utility. They force a token into something that would work better without one—like adding wings to a car and calling it an airplane.

The life cycle of a dying project is predictable. It launches with massive hype and revolutionary promises. The price pumps through paid marketing and influencer shills. Insiders who got tokens at near-zero cost dump on retail buyers at the peak. Development slows as the treasury empties into founders' pockets. The community slowly realizes they've been scammed as promises go unfulfilled. Price crashes 99%. The Telegram goes quiet. The website stops updating. Another tombstone in the graveyard.

Some projects don't even pretend to build. They're exit scams from day one, designed to extract maximum value before disappearing. Others have good intentions but no ability to execute. A great idea without execution is worthless. The result is the same either way: your money goes to zero while founders disappear with millions.

The Tokenomics Deep Dive That Reveals Everything

Tokenomics is the genetic code of every crypto project. Before evaluating anything else, understand the tokenomics completely. They determine whether a project can mathematically succeed or is doomed from genesis. This is where most investors fail. They see a low price and assume it's cheap without understanding the supply dynamics that might be making it expensive.

Start by mapping the complete supply picture. Maximum supply sets the theoretical ceiling, but it's the emission schedule that matters. A project with only 10% of tokens circulating faces 10x dilution as the remaining 90% enter the market. Those tokens don't appear randomly; they unlock on specific dates. Mark those dates on your calendar, because they often coincide with violent price dumps as insiders finally get to cash out.

Distribution reveals the true power structure. If venture capitalists bought at $0.001 and retail buys at $1, you're not an investor; you're exit liquidity. The VCs need the price to drop 99.9% before they lose money. You lose money if it drops 1%. Who do you think has stronger hands? Who's more likely to dump on the first pump?

Check team allocations with extreme skepticism. Founders taking 20% isn't necessarily bad if those tokens vest over four years with one-year cliffs. But if team tokens are already circulating while they tell the community to "hold for the long term," they're dumping on you. Watch the blockchain, not their words. Set up wallet alerts for team addresses. When they move large amounts to exchanges while posting about building, you have your answer.

Token utility determines whether holding makes sense beyond speculation. Governance tokens matter only if they govern something valuable. Voting on meaningless parameters while the team controls the multisig isn't governance; it's theater. Fee-sharing tokens need actual fees to share. If the protocol generates $10,000 annually but has a billion-dollar market cap, you're buying hope, not value.

The death spirals hide in complex tokenomics. Hyperinflationary promises of 10,000% APY come from token printing, not revenue. The price drops due to dilution, requiring even higher nominal yields to maintain dollar returns. Eventually, emission overwhelms demand and price approaches zero. Terra

Luna was worth $60 billion before this exact mechanism destroyed it in 72 hours. If you can't explain where yield comes from in one sentence, it comes from diluting you.

The Quality Assessment Framework That Actually Works

After years of wins and losses, certain patterns emerged that now help me separate quality from garbage. Quality projects share four unmistakable characteristics that become obvious once you know what to look for.

First, they solve specific problems for specific users. Not vague promises about "revolutionizing finance" or "disrupting everything." Quality projects address specific, measurable, valuable problems. Chainlink solves the oracle problem, getting real-world data onto blockchains. Uniswap enables permissionless token swaps without intermediaries. Aave facilitates decentralized lending and borrowing. The problem and the solution are immediately obvious. If it takes an essay to explain what problem is being solved, there isn't one.

Second, they generate revenue from actual usage, not token speculation. Quality projects are businesses that happen to have tokens, not tokens pretending to be businesses. Uniswap generates millions in daily trading fees. Aave earns from the spread between lending and borrowing rates. The token captures real value from real economic activity. Most projects generate nothing and never will, surviving only on the greater fool theory until the music stops.

Third, they build through bear markets when there's no hype to sustain them. Check the project's GitHub commits during the 2022 crash when everything was down 90%. Were they still pushing code daily? Or did development mysteriously stop when token prices crashed? Bear markets reveal who's here for the technology versus the money. Projects that maintain development regardless of price are positioning for the next cycle. Those that stop building when prices drop were only ever about extracting value.

Fourth, they become infrastructure that others build upon. Ethereum hosts thousands of projects. Chainlink serves hundreds of protocols. When other projects depend on yours for critical functionality, you become essential rather than optional. Network effects compound over time, creating moats that marketing can't replicate. Every project building on top makes the foundation more valuable. This is how lasting value gets created in crypto.

Red Flags That Should End Your Research Immediately

Some warnings are so reliable that seeing even one should terminate your evaluation. These aren't yellow flags suggesting caution; they're red flags signaling guaranteed disasters that will take your money.

Guaranteed returns are always scams. No exceptions. Markets fluctuate. Yields vary. Anyone promising fixed returns is either running a Ponzi or doesn't understand mathematics. Real yields come from real economic activity, which naturally fluctuates. If someone claims they've solved sustainable high fixed yields, they're lying or delusional.

Celebrity endorsements mean exit liquidity is needed. Kim Kardashian doesn't understand blockchain technology. Floyd Mayweather Jr. isn't evaluating smart contracts. They're paid millions to get liquidity from their followers, only to dump all the tokens on them later. The budget spent on one celebrity endorsement could have funded years of development. That tells you everything about priorities.

Aggressive marketing with no working product reveals a scam. Quality projects build first, market later. Scams market first because there's nothing to build. If they're spending millions on billboards, influencers, and ads but you can't find a testnet, GitHub repo, or actual usage, you're not the customer; you're the product being sold.

Team members dumping tokens while preaching "diamond hands" are showing their true intentions. The blockchain doesn't lie. When team wallets are selling while they post about long-term vision, their only vision is extracting your money. Actions reveal truth; words reveal nothing.

Your Complete Research Process

Quality research follows a systematic process that removes emotion and reveals reality. Start with a one-hour quick scan to eliminate obvious frauds. Visit their website and read the documentation. After ten minutes, do you understand what problem they're solving? If not, move on. Professional design doesn't mean legitimacy. Sloppy execution means avoid. Scammers can afford good designers, but teams that can't present their idea clearly can't execute it, either.

Read the white paper completely, not just the tokenomics section. The white paper tells you what they claim to do. Understanding it tells you if those claims make sense. Bitcoin's white paper was nine pages. Ethereum's was thirty-six. If it takes more than that to explain the value proposition, they're hiding simplicity behind complexity. Real innovations may be difficult to execute, but they are simple to explain.

Vet the team through actual evidence, not claims. Actual evidence includes real LinkedIn profiles with verifiable history, not ones that were created last month. Previous projects that were actually shipped and successful, not just announced. GitHub contributions you can verify, not just claims of experience. Pseudonymous teams aren't automatically bad—Satoshi was pseudonymous—but they need to prove competence through working code, not promises.

Check on-chain metrics for reality versus marketing. Token distribution shows who actually owns what. Transaction patterns reveal real usage versus wash trading. Revenue generation proves business model validity. The blockchain is the source of truth. Everything else is marketing. If they claim millions of users but only have thousands of on-chain transactions, they're lying.

Test the product yourself. This is where most investors fail: they invest in protocols they've never used. Actually try the product. Send transactions. Provide liquidity. Stake tokens. Whatever the protocol does, do it. You'll immediately understand whether it solves a real problem or creates unnecessary complexity. Most "revolutionary" projects are just existing solutions with extra steps and tokens forced in.

Here's a pro tip: Create a separate test wallet specifically for trying new protocols. Fund it with some gas fees and stables or whatever chain you're exploring. This is your education budget, not your investment capital. *Use this test wallet to interact with every protocol you're considering investing in.* Swap on their DEX. Stake in their pools. Try their lending markets. Go through their entire user flow. You'll quickly discover which protocols have smooth, intuitive experiences and which are clunky nightmares that no one will actually use.

This test wallet serves another purpose: protecting your main holdings. New protocols can have bugs, exploits, or malicious code. By testing with a small, separate wallet, you limit any losses to your education budget. Never connect your main wallet—the one with serious holdings—to unproven protocols.

Think of it like test-driving cars. You wouldn't buy a car without driving it first. Why would you invest thousands in a protocol you've never used? That $10 spent actually using various protocols will teach you more than reading a hundred white papers. Plus, you might discover genuinely useful tools you'll incorporate into your regular DeFi strategy.

Your Path Forward in the Graveyard

The crypto graveyard will keep growing. Thousands more projects will launch, pump, and die. But, armed with this framework, you can avoid becoming exit liquidity and instead identify the few projects that will define the future.

Remember: in crypto, the default outcome is failure. Your job isn't to find every opportunity but to identify the few that matter while avoiding the many that don't. Quality projects are rare, *maybe* 5% of what launches, but that 5% will capture 95% of the value. The Pareto Principle on steroids.

All the tools are free. The information is public. The blockchain doesn't lie. The only question is whether you'll do the work or chase the hype. A project you research thoroughly becomes a conviction. The convictions you hold through volatility become wealth. So, the next time you see revolutionary technology with celebrity endorsements and massive marketing, remember the graveyard. Twenty thousand projects that looked amazing before going to zero. Your research determines whether you visit those tombstones as a tourist learning what to avoid, or as an investor who lost everything.

15

Building Wealth Through Portfolio Design, Not Luck

Spring 2021 was my wake-up call. I'd turned $50,000 into $400,000 by going all in on altcoins during the bull run. Every coin I touched seemed to 10x. I was a genius. Untouchable. Then May happened.

Over the next few weeks, I watched $400,000 become $80,000. Not because I sold, but because I had no portfolio structure. No core holdings. No stablecoin reserves. No profit-taking plan. Just a collection of altcoins mixed with hopium. When the market crashed, my "diversified" portfolio of twenty different altcoins all crashed together. Turns out, owning twenty coins that all move in the same direction isn't diversification. It's just complicated concentration.

That expensive lesson forced me to develop an actual portfolio architecture. Not the traditional finance kind where you own 60% stocks and 40% bonds. That doesn't work in crypto, where everything can move 20% in a day. I needed something built for this market's volatility while still building long-term wealth.

The Two-Portfolio System That Changes Everything

After years of refinement, I've discovered that the optimal crypto portfolio isn't one portfolio, but rather two completely separate systems with different goals, strategies, and time horizons.

Your **holdings portfolio** is your fortress of wealth. This is Bitcoin, Ethereum, and maybe a few blue-chip cryptos you believe will dominate in ten years. You're not trading these. You're not yield-farming with these. You're holding them in cold storage, accumulating more during bear markets, and taking profits at predetermined levels during bulls. This is your "get wealthy steadily" portfolio that captures crypto's long-term appreciation.

Your **DeFi cash flow portfolio** is your income engine. This is capital deployed in DeFi strategies generating yield through liquidity provision, lending, and staking. This portfolio pays you monthly regardless of market direction. The yields either cover living expenses or, better yet, buy more assets for your holdings portfolio. We'll dive deep into these strategies in part IV, but understanding the separation is crucial now.

Most people mix these together and wonder why they're always stressed. They're trying to generate income from their long-term holdings or hoping their yield-farming positions will make them rich. That's like expecting your retirement fund to pay monthly bills or your checking account to fund retirement. Different money serves different purposes.

The separation creates clarity. When Bitcoin crashes 30%, your holdings portfolio takes the hit, but you don't panic because that's long-term money. Meanwhile, your DeFi portfolio keeps generating income, giving you capital to buy the dip. When markets pump, your holdings appreciate while your DeFi portfolio's yields might compress, but you're capturing gains from both appreciation and income.

Core Holdings: The Foundation of Your Portfolio

Your holdings portfolio should be boringly simple. These are assets that will definitely exist and likely dominate in five years. In crypto, that's a very short list. You first met this concept back in Chapter 5, where we framed the barbell strategy as 80% in established assets and 20% in higher-risk opportunities. The same principle applies here, but in a more advanced form. As your capital and experience grow, the *percentages may shift, but* not the philosophy. The goal remains the same: concentrate most of your wealth in assets built to endure (like Bitcoin and Ethereum), while keeping a small slice reserved for asymmetric opportunities that have higher upside.

Bitcoin should typically make up 50% (or more) of your total portfolio value. Not just your holdings portfolio, your entire net worth allocated to crypto. Yes, that seems high. Yes, altcoins might outperform in the short term. But Bitcoin is the reserve asset of crypto. Every institution buys Bitcoin first. Every country adopting crypto starts with Bitcoin. When crypto crashes, Bitcoin crashes least. When crypto recovers, Bitcoin leads.

The allocation seems conservative until you live through a real bear market. When altcoins are down 95%, that Bitcoin you bought that's down "only" 50% looks like genius. More importantly, Bitcoin's risk-adjusted returns beat almost everything over four-year periods. You're not sacrificing returns for safety, you're optimizing for sustainable wealth building.

Ethereum gets 20–40% of the total portfolio. Every major innovation in crypto happens on Ethereum first. DeFi, NFTs, DAOs, everything starts there. Other chains are faster and cheaper, but Ethereum has the developers, users, and network effects that matter. It's the platform everything else builds on.

The remaining 10–20% can include a few carefully selected altcoins, but this is optional. If you do venture beyond Bitcoin and Ethereum, stick to protocols that have survived multiple cycles, generate real revenue, and have become essential infrastructure. Chainlink for oracles. Aave for lending. Uniswap for trading. These aren't moonshots; they're the picks and shovels of crypto.

The key with holdings is discipline. You accumulate during bear markets when everyone's depressed. You take profits during bull markets when everyone's euphoric. You never panic-sell. You never FOMO-buy. You follow the cycles we discussed in chapter 11, not your emotions.

Position Sizing That Prevents Catastrophe

Position sizing in crypto is different than in traditional markets because correlations are higher and volatility is extreme. Traditional diversification fails when everything moves together.

Never put more than 5% of your portfolio in any single altcoin outside the top 10. Even if you're absolutely convinced it's the next Ethereum. Even if your favorite influencer is all in. Especially if everyone in your group chat owns it. Concentration creates wealth, but it also destroys it. The graveyard of crypto is full of people who went all in on "sure things."

The 1% rule saves portfolios: never put more than 1% in anything you don't fully understand. If you can't explain the tokenomics, don't know the team, or haven't used the product, keep it tiny. Consider it tuition for education. Most people lose money on investments they didn't understand but bought anyway because of FOMO.

Correlation awareness prevents fake diversification. Owning twenty DeFi tokens isn't diversification if they all pump and dump together. Real diversification means different asset types serving different functions. Bitcoin for store of value. Ethereum for smart contract exposure. Stablecoins for dry powder. DeFi positions for income. Different purposes, different risk profiles, different correlation patterns.

The Cash Flow Portfolio That Pays You

While your holdings portfolio builds long-term wealth, your DeFi cash flow portfolio generates immediate income. This is where you put capital to work, earning yield through various DeFi strategies.

Start with stablecoin lending as your baseline. USDC and USDT in established lending protocols earning 5–10% APY. Boring? Yes. Reliable? Also yes. This is your portfolio's steady income, showing up every month regardless of market conditions. During bull markets, these rates might jump to 20%+. During bears, they might drop to 3%. But they're always positive and always paying.

Blue-chip liquidity provision is where returns get interesting. ETH/USDC pools, WBTC/ETH pools, major token pairs with real volume. Using concentrated liquidity strategies we'll explore in Part IV, you can earn 50% or more APR on quality pairs. The key is choosing pairs you'd hold anyway and managing your ranges actively.

Staking yields from Ethereum and other proof-of-stake chains add another layer. ETH staking yields are typically 4–5% APY on an appreciating asset. Other chains offer higher yields but with higher risks. Match the risk to your conviction. Stake ETH because you believe in Ethereum. Don't stake random tokens just for yield.

The crucial principle: your DeFi portfolio uses different capital than your holdings. You're not lending out your long-term Bitcoin. You're not providing liquidity with your entire ETH stack. This is separate capital specifically allocated for income generation.

Risk Management Without Complex Math

Effective risk management in crypto doesn't require spreadsheets and formulas. It requires discipline and commonsense rules that you actually follow.

The sleep test determines position sizing. If you're checking prices at 3 a.m., you're over-allocated. If a 50% crash would ruin your life, you're over-leveraged. If you don't understand what you own, you're overexposed. Size your positions so you can sleep through volatility.

Time-horizon matching prevents forced selling. Money you need in six months shouldn't be in crypto. Money you need in two years shouldn't be in altcoins. Only money you won't need for 4+ years belongs in volatile assets. This prevents selling bottoms because you need cash for life expenses.

The barbell approach balances risk and reward. That means heavy allocation to the safest assets (Bitcoin/Ethereum), small bets on asymmetric opportunities, and nothing in the middle. Either maximum safety or maximum upside, no mediocre compromises. This gives you stability from core holdings and lottery tickets from small bets.

Systematic profit-taking removes emotion from selling. We'll cover the ladder-out strategy in detail in chapter 16, but the principle is simple: take profits on the way up, not after the crash. Sell into strength when everyone's buying, not into weakness when everyone's selling.

Rebalancing for Crypto Markets

Traditional yearly or quarterly rebalancing doesn't work in crypto where assets can 10x in months. Crypto requires threshold-based rebalancing triggered by price movements, not calendar dates.

When any position exceeds 2x its target allocation, trim back to 1.5x target. This lets winners run while still taking profits. If your 5% position grows to 10% of portfolio, sell enough to bring it to 7.5%. You lock in gains while maintaining exposure.

When positions fall below 0.5x their target allocation, evaluate whether to add or abandon. If the thesis remains valid and it's just market dynamics, consider adding. If the thesis broke, exit completely. Never average down on broken theses hoping for recovery.

Core holdings (Bitcoin/Ethereum) get different treatment. These you accumulate during bear markets regardless of allocation percentages. You're not rebalancing these based on price; you're following market cycles. Accumulate when everyone's depressed. Lock in profits when everyone's euphoric.

The proceeds from rebalancing have three possible destinations: stablecoins for future opportunities, adding to core holdings, or funding your DeFi portfolio. Never immediately rotate into another risky position. Take chips off the table first, then decide where to redeploy.

Your Portfolio Will Evolve as You Learn

Your portfolio should evolve with your knowledge and experience, not your risk appetite or FOMO level. Beginner portfolios should be dead simple: 60% Bitcoin, 30% Ethereum, 10% stablecoins. That's it. No altcoins, no DeFi, no complications. Learn market cycles and volatility with assets that won't go to zero. Maybe earn some yield on the stablecoins, but focus on understanding the market's rhythm first.

After surviving your first 50% drawdown without panic-selling, you can add complexity. An intermediate portfolio might be: 40% Bitcoin, 25% Ethereum, 15% blue-chip alts, 20% DeFi income strategies. Now you're capturing more upside while generating income. You understand risk management and market cycles.

Advanced portfolios maximize capital efficiency across both systems. Holdings used as collateral for borrowing. Borrowed funds deployed in yield strategies. Yields compounding into more holdings. Multiple income streams across protocols. Active management of concentrated liquidity. This requires deep understanding and constant attention but generates the highest returns.

The key is evolving gradually. Each level teaches lessons needed for the next. Rush the process, and the market will humble you expensively. The tourists who show up during bull markets with complex strategies leave with simple losses.

Also remember that separating holdings from income generation creates psychological clarity that improves decision-making. When Bitcoin's price drops, you're not worried about income because your DeFi portfolio keeps paying. When yields compress, you're not worried about short-term cash flow because your holdings keep appreciating long term.

This separation prevents the mixing of time horizons that destroys returns. You don't panic-sell holdings because you need income. You don't chase unsustainable yields hoping for appreciation. Each portfolio has its job, and you let it do that job without interference.

More importantly, separation creates multiple paths to wealth. Your holdings capture crypto's long-term appreciation. Your DeFi portfolio generates income to buy more holdings. Bull markets accelerate holdings growth. Bear markets offer accumulation opportunities funded by DeFi income. You win either way.

Start Small, Keep It Simple

Building wealth through creating a crypto portfolio isn't about finding the perfect allocation. It's about creating a system that survives bear markets and thrives in bulls while generating income throughout.

Start simple with mostly Bitcoin and Ethereum. Add complexity only as you gain experience. Separate long-term holdings from income generation.

Size positions to sleep well. Take profits systematically. Rebalance based on price, not time.

The $400,000 portfolio I nearly destroyed in 2021 taught me that framework through expensive tuition. Today, using this two-portfolio system, I grow my crypto portfolio steadily regardless of market conditions. More importantly, I sleep well knowing my systems actually gets stronger through volatility rather than breaking from it. Each market cycle, each crash, each recovery makes the system more robust because it's designed to thrive on chaos, not just survive it.

Your portfolio structure determines whether you'll survive long enough to thrive. Get the systems right, and the profits follow. Get it wrong, and no amount of good picks will save you from catastrophic failure when the inevitable crash arrives.

16

The Art of Taking Profits
Before Greed Becomes Regret

In the last chapter, I showed you how to build a two-portfolio system that survives crypto's volatility. But even the best portfolio structure means nothing if you never extract value from it. This chapter solves the other half of the wealth equation: systematically converting unrealized gains into permanent wealth.

Most crypto investors master buying but fail catastrophically at selling. They accumulate positions brilliantly, research thoroughly, time entries well… and then watch everything evaporate because they have no exit strategy. The same people who would celebrate banking a 20% gain in stocks watch 300% gains in crypto disappear without selling a single token.

You already know about my $400,000 portfolio that crashed to $80,000. What I didn't tell you was the systematic framework I developed afterward: one that ensures I never again round-trip what could have been life-changing money. This ladder-out strategy removes emotion from profit-taking, guaranteeing that you capture gains while maintaining exposure to further upside.

The problem isn't knowledge; it's psychology. Everyone knows they should take profits eventually. But when your portfolio is up 500% and crypto Twitter is calling for 2000%, selling feels like betrayal. When that coin you bought at $1 hits $10, your brain immediately anchors to $100. You become paralyzed between greed for more and fear of missing the top.

The Ladder-Out Strategy That Saves Portfolios

The laddering-out strategy solves this paralysis by creating a systematic framework for profit-taking that removes emotion from the equation. Instead of trying to time the perfect top, which is impossible, or holding forever, which is painful, you take profits incrementally as positions grow, securing gains while maintaining exposure to further upside.

Consider a $10,000 position in any crypto asset. Instead of the all-or-nothing approach that destroys most portfolios, you structure your exit like this:

Sell 20% at a 50% gain. Your $10,000 is now worth $15,000 total. Selling 20% means selling $3,000, which recovers 30% of your initial investment. You're already reducing risk.

Sell another 20% at 2x. When it doubles to $20,000 total value, selling 20% of your original position means selling another $4,000. You've now extracted $7,000 from your $10,000 investment—70% of your capital is secured.

Sell another 20% at 3x. At 3x ($30,000 total value), selling 20% means another $6,000. You've now taken $13,000 from a $10,000 investment. You're in profit no matter what happens next.

Sell another 20% at 5x if it keeps running. At 5x ($50,000 total value), that's another $10,000. You've extracted $23,000 from your initial $10,000, more than doubling your money in realized gains.

Hold the final 20% forever as your moon bag. This captures any extreme moves crypto is famous for. If it goes to zero, you've still made 2.3x on your investment. If it goes to 20x, that remaining 20% is worth another $40,000. This final piece is your lottery ticket that you never have to stress about because you've already won.

This more conservative structure ensures you start taking profits much earlier, reducing the risk of round-tripping gains. The mathematics work because you're not waiting for massive multiples to start securing profits—you begin at just 50% gains, which happen frequently in crypto.

Setting Your Ladder Levels Based on Asset Type

The art of laddering out is setting levels that match the asset's potential and your personal goals. Not all cryptocurrencies deserve the same exit strategy.

Bitcoin might use conservative targets like 20%, 40%, 80%, and 150% gains from your entry. Bitcoin remains the most stable crypto asset, but that stability means it makes sense to take profits at smaller increments. When Bitcoin gains 80%, locking in some profit is prudent because the next 80% could take months or years.

Ethereum can handle slightly more aggressive targets like 50%, 100%, 200%, and 300% gains. It has more upside than Bitcoin but also more volatility. Your ladder should capture this middle ground between stability and speculation.

Quality altcoins in the top 20 might use 100%, 200%, 500%, and even 1000% targets. These have proven themselves but still have room for significant growth, and they could realistically do 5–10x or more in a strong bull market. Your ladder should be positioned to capture these moves without waiting for unrealistic multiples.

Small-cap moonshots need more extreme targets like 3x, 10x, 20x, and 50x. If you're buying microcaps, you're hunting for asymmetric returns. But even here, taking some profit at 3x ensures you lock in gains and ride on house money rather than watching everything round-trip. Either it goes parabolic or it goes to zero, but at least you've extracted something along the way.

The key is setting these levels before entering the position, when you're rational—not during the pump, when greed dominates. Write your targets down. Put them in a spreadsheet. Make them real and immutable. Then, when emotion hits during the bull run, you're not making decisions; you're executing predetermined plans.

The Psychology That Sabotages Profit-Taking

Understanding why people fail to take profits is as important as knowing how to take them. The human brain isn't wired for exponential gains. It evolved for linear thinking in a world where 10x returns didn't exist.

Anchoring bias destroys more portfolios than any other psychological trap. Once you see your $1,000 investment hit $10,000, your brain anchors to that number. When it pulls back to $7,000, you feel like you've lost $3,000 rather than gained $6,000. You wait for recovery to $10,000 before selling, but it drops to $5,000. Now you're definitely waiting. It drops to $2,000. You've round-tripped a 10x into a 2x because your brain anchored to the peak.

The endowment effect makes you overvalue assets simply because you own them. Your coins become "special" compared to identical coins you don't own. Selling feels like losing something valuable rather than gaining realized profit. This cognitive bias intensifies the longer you hold, making profit-taking progressively harder.

Social proof amplifies these biases exponentially. When everyone on Twitter is calling for higher prices, selling feels like betrayal to the community. When influencers post price targets 10x above current levels, taking profits at 2x seems foolish. When your Discord group is euphoric, being the person who sells kills the vibe. You become trapped between personal profit and social belonging.

FOMO might be the most powerful force preventing profit-taking. What if you sell and it keeps going up? What if this is the coin that goes 1000x and you sold at 10x? What if everyone gets rich except you because you took profits "too early"? This fear paralyzes decision-making, ensuring you'll hold until it's too late.

Market Indicators That Scream "Take Profits Now"

While you shouldn't try to time the perfect top, certain indicators have proven remarkably reliable for knowing when to accelerate your ladder-out strategy:

When the Fear and Greed Index hits "Extreme Greed" above 80. Every major crypto top has followed within months of this happening. This doesn't mean sell everything immediately, but it means start executing your ladder aggressively. When everyone's greedy, be fearful. When everyone's fearful, be greedy.

When Google Trends data for "how to buy Bitcoin" or "how to buy crypto" spikes near cycle tops. When your hairdresser asks about Dogecoin, when mainstream media runs crypto segments daily, when your uncle who called Bitcoin a scam wants to invest, these social indicators are screaming at you to take profits.

When long-term holder movements tell you the smart money is selling. When addresses that haven't moved Bitcoin in years suddenly start sending to exchanges, they know something. These diamond hands don't break easily. When they do, pay attention and accelerate your profit-taking.

When blockchain data shows billions in crypto flowing into exchanges after months of outflows. Such a shift is a clear indication that holders are preparing to sell. This on-chain data doesn't lie. Marketing lies. Price predictions lie. But blockchain data shows you exactly what's actually happening.

When you're feeling euphoric. Your own emotional state might be the best indicator. When you feel invincible, when you're calculating how many Lambos you'll buy with your gains, when you're thinking about quitting your job to trade full time, that's maximum euphoria. That's when you should be selling—not planning yacht purchases.

What to Do with Profits

Taking profits is only half the equation. What you do with those profits determines whether you build lasting wealth or just temporarily touch it.

The first tranche should always secure your initial investment. This psychological milestone transforms everything else into house money. Move this to stablecoins earning yield, or even completely out of crypto. This is your "sleep well" money that ensures you can't lose overall.

Middle tranches can be more flexible. Some investors might rotate into Bitcoin or Ethereum as stable stores of value. Some might move to stablecoins earning 5-10% APY while waiting for the next opportunity. Some might fund real-world purchases that improve their lives. The key is having a plan before the profits arrive.

Never immediately rotate profits into another speculative position. This is how people turn winning trades into losing portfolios. Take the chips off the table first. Let them cool in stablecoins or Bitcoin. Then, when you're calm and the market has cooled, decide where to redeploy.

Also, consider the tax implications before they surprise you. In most jurisdictions, every sale is a taxable event. Setting aside 20–40% of profits for taxes prevents the nightmare of owing more than you have. The worst outcome is making massive profits, losing them in the bear market, then owing taxes on gains that no longer exist.

The Positions You Never Sell

While laddering out captures profits systematically, certain positions deserve different treatment. Your core Bitcoin and Ethereum holdings from your holdings portfolio might never be fully sold, only partially trimmed during extreme euphoria.

These forever holds represent your bet on crypto's long-term future. They're not trades; they're wealth storage. You might ladder out 50% during bull markets but always maintain core positions. This ensures you're never completely out of the game when crypto achieves its full potential. And you can use the profits to simply buy back more when prices pull back.

The moon bags you build from your laddered positions may also join this never-sell category. These are your lottery tickets for the scenarios where crypto truly revolutionizes finance. If Bitcoin hits $1 million or Ethereum powers the global financial system, these positions ensure you participate in that upside.

Building Your Personal Exit System

Creating your exit strategy starts with brutal honesty about your goals and psychology. Are you investing for retirement in 20 years, or are you trying to buy a house next year? Can you handle watching a position continue up after selling, or will you FOMO back in at the top? Your strategy must match *your* temperament, not someone else's.

Write down your ladder levels before buying anything. This simple act transforms hopeful gambling into systematic investing. When emotions hit during bull markets, you're not making decisions; you're executing predetermined plans.

Start simple with your first few exits: maybe just sell 10% every time something goes up by 20%. Once comfortable with basic laddering, add complexity. Different percentages, different multiples, different strategies for different assets. Evolution through experience beats complex theories.

Track and journal every exit to improve your process. Did you sell too early? Too late? Did emotions override your plan? Each exit teaches you about your psychology and helps you refine your strategy. The goal isn't perfection but continuous improvement toward systematic wealth building.

No FOMO, There Is Always Another Opportunity

Here's the truth that took me years to internalize: crypto never stops creating opportunities. Every cycle brings new projects, new innovations, new chances to build wealth. The fear that you're "missing out" by taking profits is an illusion created by scarcity mindset.

Crypto is an infinite game, not a finite one. There isn't one chance to get rich that disappears forever if you sell. Every month brings new protocols launching, new narratives emerging, new cycles beginning. The DeFi summer of 2020 created fortunes. Then NFTs in 2021 created new fortunes. Then Layer 2s. Then AI tokens. The opportunities never stop coming.

Selling "too early" with 3x profits is infinitely better than holding for 10x and watching it crash back to break-even. Those realized 3x gains become the seed capital for your next 5x, which becomes the capital for the next 10x. Compound realized gains beat theoretical returns every time.

Remember that the market will always give you another opportunity to enter. New projects launch daily. Bear markets create buying opportunities regularly. Innovation never stops. But the market rarely gives you another chance to exit at the top. When you have profits, take them. **When gains are real, lock them in.**

Part IV:

Becoming Your Own Bank

17

Building Your Own
Financial System with DeFi

The mortgage application was supposed to be straightforward. I had three years of steady income from the oil rigs, okay savings, decent credit. I was trying to buy a modest condo, nothing fancy. Just wanted to stop burning money on rent and build some equity.

The loan officer smiled that practiced smile that means nothing. "We'll need to verify your employment history." Six weeks later, still verifying. Apparently, three years of T4s and bank statements showing consistent deposits weren't enough.

Two months in: "Your employment type is considered high risk." High risk? I'd been working steadily for three years, never missed a payment on anything, had 20% down ready to go. But because I worked on rigs that oftentimes had seasonal work instead of sitting in an office, I was "high risk."

Three months in: "We can approve you, but you'll need 20% down or more and mortgage insurance." They were literally making me pay extra to insure them against the risk that I, the person who'd never missed a payment, might miss a payment.

The whole process took four months. Four months of documents, meetings, phone calls, and justifying why someone who worked in brutal conditions deserved the privilege of owing the bank money. By the end, I felt like I should have thanked them for the opportunity to pay them interest.

Years later, I discovered DeFi. No applications. No judgmental loan officers. No employment verification. Just code that treats everyone exactly the same. The contrast was so stark, it changed how I see everything about money and power.

The Banking Scam Hidden in Plain Sight

Traditional banks operate on a model so elegant in its extraction that once you see it, you can't unsee it. They take your money, pay you nothing (maybe 0.05% if you're lucky), then lend it out at 5% to 25%. They pocket the difference while acting like they're doing you a favor by "keeping your money safe."

But here's the part that should make you angry: it's *your* money they're lending. You take all the inflation risk while they take all the profit. Your purchasing power erodes at 7% annually while they pay you 0.05% and lend your money for 20% on credit cards. And if you want to borrow your own money back? Four months of paperwork and maybe they'll consider it.

The first time I used DeFi, this entire charade fell apart. I had a few thousand USDC sitting idle in my wallet. I connected to Aave, a decentralized lending protocol. No application. No credit check. No questions about my employment history. I simply deposited my USDC.

The entire process took thirty seconds. Documentation required: zero. Permission needed: none. Interest rate: 8.2% APY at the time. But what really blew my mind was the transparency. I could see everything. The smart contract code was public, auditable by anyone. Interest rates updated in real-time based on actual supply and demand, not some arbitrary decision by a bank executive. Every transaction visible on the blockchain. No hidden fees. No backroom deals.

For the first time in my life, I was interacting with a financial system that couldn't discriminate against me. The code treats everyone exactly the same, whether you're depositing $100 or $100 million.

You're Not Using Better Banking, You're Replacing Banking

Here's what most people don't understand about DeFi until it clicks: you're not accessing better financial services. You're becoming the financial service. When you deposit into Aave or Compound, you're not giving your money to a company. You're adding liquidity to a protocol. When someone borrows, they're borrowing from the pool you're part of. You get the interest. Not some CEO. Not shareholders. You.

Think about what this means. Every loan, every trade, every financial service that banks charge billions for, you can now participate in providing these services and earning the fees. You've gone from being the product to being the owner.

In traditional finance, you have no idea what your bank does with your deposits. They could be funding oil wars, private prisons, or their CEO's yacht collection. In DeFi, every transaction is visible. You can see exactly where every dollar goes, how it's used, and what yield it generates.

This transparency creates accountability that traditional finance can never match. Bad actors get exposed immediately. Unsustainable yields collapse quickly. Only protocols that actually work survive long term. It's financial Darwinism in real time.

The Compound Effect That Banks Don't Want You to Understand

Let me show you math that banks pray you never understand. Traditional savings account: 0.05% APY. After inflation at 7%, you're actually losing 6.95% annually. Your $10,000 becomes worth $9,305 in real purchasing power after one year. You're literally paying the bank to make you poorer.

DeFi stablecoin lending: 8% APY currently. After the same 7% inflation, you're gaining 1% in real terms. Not amazing, but you're preserving wealth instead of destroying it.

But here's where it gets interesting. DeFi yields compound automatically, sometimes daily or even per block (every 12 seconds on Ethereum). Traditional banks compound monthly if you're lucky, annually if you're not. This difference seems small but compounds into massive gaps over time.

More importantly, in DeFi you can stack yields. Lend your USDC for 8%, take that yield and provide liquidity for 20%, take those fees and stake them for 15%. Suddenly you're not making 8%. You're compounding yields on yields on yields. Banks do this exact strategy with your money. They just keep all the profits. DeFi lets you be the one running the strategy.

How Lending and Borrowing Actually Work in DeFi

The mechanics are elegantly simple once you understand them. Lending protocols are just pools of capital with programmed rules. You deposit assets into the pool. Others borrow from the pool. Interest paid by borrowers goes to lenders. No middleman. No bank taking 90% of the spread.

When you deposit $10,000 USDC into Aave, you receive aUSDC tokens representing your share of the pool. As borrowers pay interest, your aUSDC becomes redeemable for more USDC. The interest compounds every block, about every 12 seconds. You can withdraw anytime. No penalties. No lock-ups. No asking permission.

LENDERS   **BORROWERS**

Borrowing is equally revolutionary. Instead of selling your ETH to pay for something, you can borrow against it. Deposit $10,000 of ETH, borrow $5,000 USDC against it. You maintain your ETH exposure while accessing liquidity. If ETH doubles, you still benefit. Try explaining that concept to a traditional bank.

The system maintains safety through overcollateralization. You can typically borrow 50–75% of your collateral value. If your collateral value drops toward your loan value, you get liquidated to protect lenders. It's harsh, but it's fair, transparent, and automatic. No subjective decisions. Just math.

The Risks You Need to Understand

DeFi isn't risk-free magic money. Understanding the risks is the difference between building wealth and losing everything.

Smart contract risk is real. Code can have bugs. Protocols can be hacked. Always use established protocols that have been battle-tested with billions of dollars and professionally audited multiple times. Aave, Compound, and MakerDAO have proven themselves. Random new protocols promising 1000% APY have not.

Liquidation risk when borrowing requires careful management. If your collateral drops in value, you can be liquidated instantly. Never borrow more than 50% of your collateral value. Monitor your positions. Have a plan for adding collateral if needed. The protocol doesn't care about your circumstances. It just executes code.

Stablecoin risk exists even with the best stablecoins. USDC and USDT have proven stable, but they're still crypto assets. DAI is decentralized but complex. Understand what you're holding. The 20% yield on some random algorithmic stablecoin isn't worth the risk of it going to zero.

Transaction costs on Ethereum mainnet can impact returns on smaller positions. During periods of high network activity, fees for complex DeFi operations might reach $20–50, making positions under $500 less practical. This is why Layer 2 solutions like Arbitrum, Base, and Optimism are game changers, reducing fees to cents. We'll cover these in chapter 22.

Your DeFi Journey Starts Here

After years of expensive mistakes and eventual success, here's the path that I believe works best for building a DeFi income engine:

Start with education. This isn't optional. DeFi will punish ignorance harder than any financial system ever created. Read every chapter in this section twice. Understand the concepts before risking real money. Take our free DeFi course at www.TheDeFiUniversity.com. Dive into our YouTube videos at https://youtube.com/@cryptolabsresearch.

Next, do some simple lending. Deposit stablecoins into Aave or Compound. Start with $100 to understand the mechanics. Watch your balance grow every day. Get comfortable with the interfaces and transactions. This alone beats any bank by 100x.

Once you're earning steady yields from lending, explore borrowing. Instead of selling your crypto, use it as collateral to borrow stablecoins. This maintains your upside exposure while accessing liquidity. Start with very conservative loan-to-value ratios.

Graduate to liquidity provision once you understand lending. This is where yields get interesting, but it's also where complexity increases. We'll cover this extensively in the next chapter. While learning, stick to stablecoin pairs to avoid impermanent loss.

Throughout this journey, focus on sustainable yields, not unsustainable promises. The boring 10–40% APY strategies that have worked for years beat the 1000% APY farms that collapse in weeks. Compound returns from proven protocols beat gambling on unproven ones.

Also remember that DeFi isn't just about better interest rates. It's about fundamentally changing your relationship with money and power. In traditional finance, you ask permission. In DeFi, you take action. In traditional finance, rules mysteriously benefit banks. In DeFi, code is law and applies equally to everyone.

Every time you use DeFi, you're voting with your capital against a system designed to extract value from you. You're saying "I don't need you" to every bank that ever denied you, overcharged you, or treated you like a second-class citizen.

The mortgage that took four months? In DeFi, I can borrow against my crypto collateral in four minutes. That savings account paying 0.05%? My

DeFi positions average 20–50% APY across various strategies—not from speculation or gambling, but from providing actual financial services that people need and use every day.

This power also isn't reserved just for the wealthy or connected. It's available to anyone with internet access and willingness to learn. The same protocols I use are available to someone in Bangladesh, Nigeria, or suburban Kansas. Same rates. Same opportunities. Same access to freedom.

But, know this: With this power comes responsibility. DeFi is powerful enough to transform your finances and dangerous enough to destroy them if you're careless. There's no customer service number to call when you make a mistake. No reversing transactions sent to the wrong address. No recovering funds from hacked protocols.

Your Action Plan for Becoming Your Own Bank

The path from traditional finance prisoner to DeFi participant is clear but requires dedication. Start by finishing this entire section of the book. Understanding these concepts intellectually before risking capital saves expensive mistakes.

Open accounts on established DeFi protocols. Aave and Compound for lending. Uniswap for trading. Start with tiny amounts to learn the interfaces. Make mistakes with $10, not $10,000. You can find a list of trusted protocols over on www.DeFiBuddy.io.

Build your positions gradually. As you gain confidence and understanding, increase your allocation. Most people find 20–30% of their crypto portfolio in DeFi strategies provides good income without excessive risk. We've worked with clients who were 100% DeFi, which can also work, but it all depends on your overall goals and targets. You can also borrow against your crypto holdings, instantly unlocking liquidity for use in your DeFi portfolio.

Stay educated as the space evolves. DeFi moves fast. New protocols, strategies, and opportunities emerge constantly. But the fundamentals you're learning here will serve you regardless of how the space evolves. If you're interested in staying on the cutting edge of DeFi, you may consider joining our Underdog

Investor Group. You can learn more about our community over at www. UnderdogInvestorGroup.com.

The banks denied my mortgage application because I worked on oil rigs instead of in an office. Today, I earn more from DeFi than I ever made freezing on those rigs. Not because I'm special or smart. Because I learned to use protocols that treat everyone the same. And that same opportunity waits for you. The same protocols are available. The only difference between the people succeeding in DeFi and the people sitting on the sidelines is education and action. Your financial freedom doesn't require anyone's permission. It just requires you to start.

18

DeFi Basics:
Yield Farming and Liquidity Provision
Made Simple

Summer 2020. DeFi Summer, they called it. Everyone was drunk on yield, and I was no exception. I'd just discovered that regular people could provide liquidity to decentralized exchanges and earn fees from every trade. After years of paying fees to banks, brokers, and exchanges, I could finally be on the receiving end. I could be the house.

My first liquidity position was a disaster disguised as opportunity. Some random farm token paired with ETH was promising 2,000% APY. I threw in $10,000, already calculating my $200,000 annual return. Within 48 hours, the farm token crashed 90%. But here's what I didn't understand: as the price fell, traders were happily buying my ETH and giving me worthless farm tokens in return. I'd become the exit liquidity for everyone dumping their bags. That 2,000% APY meant nothing when the principal went to zero.

After losing thousands chasing unsustainable yields on garbage pairs, I finally asked myself the right question: What's the point of earning high APYs if you lose everything to token collapse? That question changed everything about how I approach liquidity provision. Today, I earn a consistent 20–50% APY on blue-chip pairs using strategies we'll build up to throughout this chapter.

Becoming the Casino Instead of the Gambler

For your entire financial life, you've been on the wrong side of the trade. When you exchange currencies at the airport, banks pocket the spread. When you trade stocks, market makers capture the bid–ask difference. When you swap tokens on Coinbase, they're earning fees on your activity. You're always the customer, never the house.

Traditional finance keeps market-making exclusive. Want to be a market maker on the NYSE? You need millions in capital, specialized licenses, and institutional connections. Want to earn foreign exchange spreads? Become a bank. The infrastructure that generates the most consistent profits is locked away from regular people.

But DeFi changed everything. Through liquidity pools, anyone with $100 can become the market maker. You provide the liquidity that enables trades, and you earn the fees that banks used to monopolize. It's the democratization of financial infrastructure.

The mental shift required is profound. Instead of trying to time the market and trade profitably, you become the market itself. Instead of paying fees, you collect them. Instead of hoping your tokens appreciate, you earn income regardless of price direction. You stop being the gambler and start being the casino.

How Liquidity Pools Actually Work

Let's start with the basics before we dive into strategies. A liquidity pool is just a smart contract holding two tokens that traders can swap between. When you add liquidity, you deposit both tokens in equal value. In return, you get LP tokens representing your share of the pool.

Every trade that happens in the pool pays a fee, typically between 0.05% to 0.3% or more. These fees don't go to some company; they stay in the pool, increasing its value. As an LP token holder, you own a percentage of this growing pool. When you withdraw, you get your share of tokens plus all accumulated fees.

The magic is in the automated market maker (AMM) formula. Instead of order books like traditional exchanges, AMMs use a simple equation: x × y = k. The product of the two token quantities always remains constant. When someone buys token x, they add y to the pool and remove x, changing the ratio and therefore the price.

This elegant system means there's always liquidity available for any trade size. The price impact just gets larger with bigger trades. And you, as the liquidity provider, earn fees from every single swap.

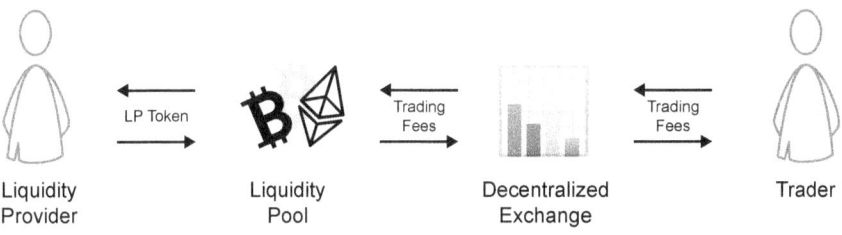

Liquidity Provider   LP Token   Liquidity Pool   Trading Fees   Decentralized Exchange   Trading Fees   Trader

Full-Range Liquidity: Your Training Wheels

In this chapter, we're focusing on full-range liquidity provision, the foundation every DeFi investor needs to understand. This is like Uniswap V2–style pools where your liquidity covers all possible prices from zero to infinity. It's simpler, more forgiving, and perfect for learning the mechanics.

Think of full-range liquidity like owning a convenience store that's always open. You might not be maximally efficient with your inventory, but you're always earning because you're always available. Some of your capital sits idle at extreme prices, but you never miss a sale.

The trade-off is clear: lower capital efficiency, but zero maintenance. You don't need to monitor positions, adjust ranges, or rebalance constantly. You just deposit, earn fees, and compound. For beginners, this simplicity is invaluable. Learn the basics here before attempting the advanced concentrated liquidity strategies we'll cover in chapter 21.

Starting with Stable Pairs

Your first liquidity position should be boringly safe: stablecoin pairs. USDC/USDT, USDC/DAI, or similar combinations. These pairs have virtually zero impermanent loss because both assets track the same dollar value. When USDC is $1.00 and USDT is $0.99, arbitrageurs trade until they're equal again, generating fees for you without changing your asset values.

The APYs on stable pairs seem modest, usually 5–15%, but this is pure profit with minimal risk. No impermanent loss. No token price risk. Just fees accumulating from the constant arbitrage that keeps stablecoins pegged.

Here's a real example from last month: $10,000 in USDC/USDT on Uniswap V2 earned roughly $75 in fees over 30 days. That's 0.75% monthly, which compounds to about 9.4% annually. Compare that to a savings account at 0.05% APY where you'd earn just $5 per year on the same $10,000. And during volatile periods, when people flee to stables, these yields can spike significantly higher.

Start here. Deploy $100–1,000 in a stablecoin pair. Watch fees accumulate daily. Get comfortable with the mechanics. Understand how to add liquidity, claim fees, and remove liquidity. Master the basics before moving to volatile pairs.

Graduating to Blue-Chip Pairs

Once you've successfully managed a stable pair for a few weeks, you're ready for volatile pairs. But not the farm token garbage that destroyed my first positions. Blue-chip pairs with real volume and sustainable demand.

ETH/USDC is the gold standard. Massive daily volume means consistent fees. Both assets have proven staying power. Yes, you'll experience impermanent loss when ETH price changes, but the fee generation often compensates. This is where the real learning begins.

When you provide ETH/USDC liquidity, you're essentially betting that trading fees will exceed impermanent loss. During sideways markets, this is almost guaranteed. During trending markets, it depends on volume. We'll dive deep into impermanent loss in the next chapter, but for now, understand that it's not actually a loss unless you withdraw at unfavorable ratios.

WBTC/ETH is another excellent training pair. These assets generally move together, reducing impermanent loss while capturing fees from ratio trades. When ETH outperforms BTC, traders swap. When BTC leads, they swap back. You earn from both directions.

Reading the Metrics That Matter

Not all pools are created equal. Before providing liquidity, you need to evaluate whether fees will compensate for risks. Here are the metrics that actually matter:

Volume-to-TVL ratio tells you how efficiently the pool generates fees. A pool with $1 million daily volume and $10 million TVL (total value locked) has a 0.1 ratio. Higher ratios mean more fees per dollar provided. Anything above 0.5 is excellent. Below 0.1 might not overcome impermanent loss.

Historical APY data shows consistency. A pool showing 50% APY today but 5% last week is probably experiencing temporary volume that won't last. Look for pools with steady yields over months, not days.

Token quality matters more than APY. A 1,000% APY on a farm token heading to zero is worse than 20% on ETH/USDC. Only provide liquidity for tokens you'd be comfortable holding independently.

Common Beginner Mistakes to Avoid

After watching hundreds of newcomers learn liquidity provision, I can tell you that the same expensive mistakes appear repeatedly. Here's how to avoid them.

The highest APY is usually a trap. Those 1000% yields that catch your eye come from hyperinflationary tokens that crash faster than you earn fees. A token printing 10% daily to pay your rewards will be worthless within weeks. Sustainable 10–50% yields on quality pairs beat unsustainable 1000% yields that evaporate your principal. Chase quality, not percentages.

Small positions need careful fee consideration. On Ethereum mainnet, entering and exiting a $500 liquidity position might cost $20 or more total during busy periods, eating into returns. This is why starting on Layer 2s like Arbitrum, Base, or Optimism is essential. The same position costs pennies to enter and exit, letting your actual yields compound instead of paying for transactions.

Providing liquidity for mystery tokens is gambling with extra steps. If you can't explain why a token has value and who's buying it, you're not investing—you're hoping. When that token inevitably crashes to zero (and most do), the fees you earned become irrelevant. Only provide liquidity for assets you understand and would hold individually.

Ignoring impermanent loss creates dangerous false confidence. That 40% APY looks amazing until you realize you're down 30% from IL, making your real return 10%. Many liquidity providers don't even know they're losing money because they only track fees, not total position value. We'll cover IL tracking in detail next chapter, but start recording your entry ratios now. The ratio between your two assets when you enter the pool becomes your benchmark for measuring true performance.

Your Full-Range LP Action Plan

Here's your exact path to becoming a successful liquidity provider, broken into manageable steps that build knowledge systematically while minimizing risk:

Week 1: Education and foundation. Before deploying a single dollar, invest in understanding. Read this chapter twice, taking notes on concepts that confuse you. Watch tutorials on providing liquidity. We have a complete series at https://youtube.com/@cryptolabsresearch that walks through every major platform. Most importantly, understand how this fits into your overall portfolio strategy: keeping your long-term holdings intact while generating cash flow on top.

Set up your tracking infrastructure now. You can track everything manually if you prefer spreadsheets, but we've built a free portfolio tracker at www. DeFiBuddy.io that automatically calculates your yields, tracks your positions across protocols, and shows your total portfolio performance. You can also get free resources and step-by-step guidance at www.TheDeFiUniversity.com.

Week 2: Stable pair experimentation. Deploy $100–500 in USDC/USDT or USDC/DAI on a platform like Uniswap or Curve. Choose Layer 2s like Arbitrum or Base, where gas costs won't eat your returns. This isn't about making money, at least not yet. It's about understanding the process. How do you add liquidity? How do you claim fees? How do you remove liquidity? Track fees daily, even if they're just pennies. This safe environment lets you make mistakes cheaply while generating your first passive income.

Weeks 3–4: Monitor, learn, and calculate. Now comes the essential part: understanding your cash flow. Check your position daily. How much did you earn today? How does weekend volume compare to weekday? Calculate your actual APY including all costs. Most people have no idea if they're actually profitable. Don't be most people. Use DeFiBuddy.io or your own tracking to know exactly what you're earning.

Month 2: Graduate to volatile pairs. Once you're comfortable with the mechanics, add $500–1000 to a blue-chip volatile pair like ETH/USDC or WBTC/ETH. This is where you start building a portfolio with multiple income streams. Maybe you keep your Bitcoin and Ethereum as long-term holdings, borrow stablecoins against them, and use those stables to provide liquidity. Now you have appreciation potential from your holdings *and* fee income from LP positions.

Month 3: Optimize and scale. Based on two months of real data, structure your complete DeFi portfolio. Maybe 40% stays in long-term holdings you never touch, another 30% generates steady income through stable pairs, and the final 30% pursues higher yields in volatile pairs. Whatever mix works for you, you're now earning cash flow while maintaining upside exposure.

Start scaling gradually. If you began with $500 and are comfortable, move to $2,000. Then $5,000. Then $10,000. Each level teaches new lessons about portfolio management and tax implications.

Month 4 and beyond: The complete system. By now, you're executing a complete portfolio strategy. Your long-term holdings appreciate over cycles. Your LP positions generate daily cash flow. You're reinvesting fees strategically, maybe into more LP positions for compound growth, or accumulating for the next bull run.

This is the power of DeFi: you don't have to choose between holding for appreciation and generating income. You can structure a portfolio that does both. Keep your Bitcoin and Ethereum for the long term. Use a portion of your portfolio or borrowed stables to generate fees. Reinvest those fees into building even larger positions.

When structured properly, you maintain full exposure to crypto's upside while generating income that rivals traditional dividend stocks. You're no longer just hoping prices go up, you're earning and stacking regardless of market direction. The fees you earn this month become next month's investment capital. The house always wins, and now you're the house—and you're using those winnings to build an even bigger house!

Setting the Foundation for Advanced Strategies

Everything you're learning with full-range liquidity becomes the foundation for advanced strategies. The concepts of fee generation, impermanent loss, and pool dynamics remain constant. Only the complexity increases.

In chapter 21, we'll explore concentrated liquidity where you can 10x your capital efficiency by providing liquidity in specific price ranges. But that requires active management and deep understanding of the basics you're learning here.

We'll also cover advanced yield strategies like delta-neutral farming, where you hedge impermanent loss while capturing fees. But, again, you need to understand basic liquidity provision first.

Think of full-range liquidity as learning to drive in a parking lot. It's safe, it's controlled, and it builds fundamental skills. Concentrated liquidity is like racing on a track. More profitable but requires mastery of basics.

You've Now Become the Bank

Successful liquidity providers think differently than traders. Traders try to predict direction; liquidity providers profit from activity. Traders want volatility in their favor; liquidity providers want volatility in any direction. Traders compete with each other; liquidity providers serve them all. When you internalize this shift, market movements stop stressing you. Bitcoin crashing? You're earning fees from panic sellers. Ethereum mooning? You're earning fees from FOMO buyers. Sideways crab market? Perfect for fee generation without impermanent loss.

You become emotionally neutral to price action because you profit regardless. This psychological shift is as valuable as the financial returns. You stop checking prices obsessively. You stop trying to time markets. You just provide liquidity and let the mathematics work. The same volatility that destroys directional traders becomes your income stream.

The path from customer to infrastructure provider isn't complex, but it requires patience and discipline. Start with education. Understand how AMMs work, what drives fees, and when impermanent loss matters. Progress to stable pairs where IL is minimal. Graduate to blue-chip volatile pairs like ETH/USDC once you understand the mechanics. Scale what works, abandon what doesn't.

Most importantly, resist the siren song of unsustainable yields. The boring 20% APY on ETH/USDC that lasts for years beats the 2000% APY that disappears in days. Compound consistency beats gambling on moonshots. Every cycle, new LPs chase the highest numbers and lose everything. Don't be them.

In the next chapter, we'll dive deep into impermanent loss, the cost of providing liquidity. You'll learn when IL matters, when it doesn't, and how to strategically manage it. But for now, focus on understanding that you can now be the house. The same fees that exchanges and banks monopolized for centuries are available to anyone with an internet connection. The revolution isn't that fees exist… it's that *you* can now earn them. So start small. Learn constantly. Scale gradually. The house always wins in the long run, and now you can be the house.

19

Impermanent Loss Explained (And How to Avoid It)

Let me warn you up front: this chapter may hurt your brain. Impermanent loss is one of those concepts that seem simple, then become confusing, then suddenly click all at once. Don't feel bad if you need to read sections twice. I've been in DeFi for years and still sometimes grab a calculator to double-check my understanding.

But here's why mastering this matters: impermanent loss isn't the portfolio killer everyone claims it is. Once you understand how it really works, it becomes a manageable cost of generating substantial income. The fear around impermanent loss keeps most people from ever providing liquidity. They see that scary word *loss* and run away. Meanwhile, those who understand what's actually happening are quietly earning 20–50% APY.

What Impermanent Loss Actually Is

Impermanent loss occurs when you provide liquidity to a pool and the price ratio of your deposited tokens changes compared to when you deposited them. The bigger the price divergence, the bigger the difference compared to just holding.

It's called "impermanent" because the loss only becomes real if you withdraw your liquidity at a price ratio different from the one at which you entered. If prices return to their original ratio, the loss disappears. Some call it "divergence loss," which is more accurate since you experience a loss relative to holding when prices diverge.

But here's what most people miss: this "loss" isn't always a bad thing. It's the cost of earning trading fees. Think of it like a store owner accepting credit cards. Yes, they pay 3% processing fees, but they make far more from increased sales. Similarly, you might experience 10% impermanent loss but earn 40% in fees.

The Mechanics in Plain English

Let's walk through what actually happens inside a liquidity pool, because most explanations get this fundamentally wrong.

You have $2,000 to provide liquidity. The ETH/USDC pool requires 50/50 value, so you deposit 1 ETH worth $1,000 and 1,000 USDC worth $1,000. Total value: $2,000.

Now ETH doubles to $2,000. Here's what actually happens: the pool doesn't "rebalance" itself. Instead, traders buy ETH from the pool with USDC. Each trade adds USDC and removes ETH, shifting the ratio until the pool price matches the market price.

After this trading activity, you now have approximately 0.707 ETH worth $1,414 and 1,414 USDC worth $1,414. Total value: $2,828.

If you'd just held, you'd have $3,000 (1 ETH at $2,000 plus $1,000 USDC). The difference of $172 is your impermanent loss, about 5.7%.

But here's the crucial insight: this ratio shift happened because traders were buying ETH from your pool. You were the seller providing liquidity, earning 0.3% on every trade. During a doubling of price, the volume can be massive. You might earn 10–20% in fees while experiencing 5.7% impermanent loss.

The Math That Actually Matters

The impermanent loss at different price ratios follows a predictable pattern:

1.5x price change = 2% loss

2x price change = 5.7% loss
3x price change = 13.4% loss
5x price change = 25.5% loss

These numbers sound scary until you realize what they represent. If ETH goes from $2,000 to $10,000 (a 5x), you experience 25% divergence loss. But you're still up 300% instead of 400%. Plus you earned fees from all the trading volume during that massive movement.

The key question isn't "Will I experience impermanent loss?" It's "Will my fees exceed my impermanent loss?" In high-volume pools, the answer is almost always yes.

When Impermanent Loss Doesn't Matter

There are several scenarios where impermanent loss becomes less important, irrelevant, or even beneficial to your overall strategy:

Stable pairs have virtually zero impermanent loss. USDC/USDT might fluctuate between 0.99 and 1.01, creating tiny divergence but generating consistent arbitrage fees. Every time Tether briefly depegs by a penny, arbitrage bots trade through your pool, paying you fees to restore the peg. This is free money with minimal risk—you're earning 5–15% APY on what's essentially a cash position. During market crashes, when everyone flees to stables, volume can spike 10x, temporarily boosting your yields to 30%+ annually.

Perfectly correlated pairs like ETH/stETH move together because they represent the same underlying asset. The impermanent loss is minimal because both assets track the same value. When stETH trades at a 0.5% discount to ETH, arbitrageurs fix it, paying you fees. You're earning from tiny price discrepancies without significant divergence risk. These pairs can often generate 10–20% returns!

Mean-reverting pairs like ETH/BTC tend to oscillate in a predictable range over time. ETH/BTC has bounced between 0.03 and 0.08 for years. You might experience temporary impermanent loss when the ratio moves, but historically it returns to the mean. Meanwhile, you're earning fees constantly from traders betting on direction. Over a full cycle, the impermanent loss often nets to near zero while fees compound.

High-fee pools can overcome impermanent loss through pure volume. A pool earning 100% APY in fees can handle 25% impermanent loss and still deliver 75% net returns. New token launches, volatile memecoins, or pools with high trading activity generate so many fees that IL can become irrelevant. Even if one asset drops 50% relative to the other, if you've earned 200% in fees you're still massively profitable.

The key insight is that impermanent loss is only "loss" if you need to exit at an unfavorable ratio. If you're providing liquidity as a long-term income strategy rather than as a trade, temporary divergence doesn't matter. The fees keep flowing regardless.

The Automatic Profit-Taking Machine

Here's what's brilliant about how pools work: they automatically take profits on the way up and can buy dips on the way down, executing the perfect trading strategy that human emotions usually sabotage.

When ETH pumps from $2,000 to $4,000, your pool doesn't just hold and hope. At $2,100, it sells a tiny bit of ETH for USDC. At $2,200, it sells a bit more. By the time ETH reaches $4,000, your pool has been taking profits at every single price point. We're talking hundreds of micro sales that add up to significant profit-taking. You're not trying to time the exact top; you're systematically selling into strength across the entire move.

When ETH falls from $4,000 back to $2,000, the process reverses. At $3,900, your pool buys a little ETH with the USDC it accumulated. At $3,800, it buys more. All the way down, it's accumulating ETH at progressively better prices. You're not trying to catch a falling knife at one specific price; you're dollar-cost averaging down through the entire correction.

This happens without any action on your part. No watching charts. No emotional decisions. No second-guessing. The AMM mechanism executes this strategy automatically through trader interactions. While traders panic-sell at the bottom and FOMO-buy at the top, your pool is doing the opposite. It's selling to them at peaks and buying from them at troughs.

Many of our Underdog Investor community members have discovered this strategy and use it as their primary method for position management. Instead of agonizing over when to take profits or buy dips, they use LP positions to automate the entire process. One member started with 20 ETH in an ETH/USDC concentrated liquidity pool (which we'll cover in detail in chapter 21). As ETH pumped higher and higher, the pool automatically sold his ETH for USDC at every price level. Eventually, the price went so high that his position went completely out of range, and he was 100% in USDC, having been automatically converted by the pool's rebalancing mechanism.

When he exited the LP position fully in stables, he sat on those USDC and waited. Once the euphoria subsided and ETH crashed 50% from its peak, he was able to buy back 30 ETH with all the profits his LP had automatically captured on the way up. The pool had forced him to take profits he never would have taken manually, turning 20 ETH into 30 ETH by using the concentrated liquidity position as an automated profit-taking mechanism during the bull run.

This beats any manual trading strategy because it removes the hardest part: actually pulling the trigger to sell during euphoria. Most holders watch their ETH go from $1,000 to $4,000 and back to $1,500 without selling a single coin. The LP forces disciplined profit-taking at every price level on the way up, giving you the dry powder to buy significantly more at the bottom. While this example uses concentrated liquidity for maximum capital efficiency, even traditional full-range pools provide this automatic rebalancing benefit, just with less dramatic results.

Think about your own trading history. How many times have you watched ETH pump to $4,000, thought "I should take some profits," but held on hoping for $5,000, only to watch it crash back to $2,500? How many times have you wanted to buy the dip but paralyzed yourself trying to time the exact bottom? The pool doesn't have these psychological barriers. It has no fear, no greed, no ego. It executes systematically at every price point, while earning you daily fees. It's a win–win!

Another client uses this strategy specifically for accumulation. When markets are getting greedy, they provide liquidity to BTC/USDC pools on the high side of their range (again, we'll get into concentrated liqiudity in chapter 21), letting the pool automatically accumulate Bitcoin as prices fall. Not only are they earning more Bitcoin while in range, they're accumulating Bitcoin at cheaper and cheaper prices. Once markets settle down, they end up with more Bitcoin than they started with, plus all the fees earned along the way. It's dollar-cost averaging perfected through liquidity pools rather than emotion.

The beauty is that this strategy aligns perfectly with long-term wealth building. You're never all in on one asset or all out in cash. You always maintain exposure to upside while continuously taking profits. You're always ready to buy dips with the stables you've accumulated. It's the balanced approach every investment advisor recommends but few investors can actually execute because emotions get in the way.

Strategies to Minimize Impermanent Loss

While impermanent loss is often acceptable given the fee income, smart positioning can minimize it and maximize your net returns:

Choose pairs wisely based on correlation and utility. Start with stable pairs like USDC/USDT or USDC/DAI where impermanent loss is nearly impossible. These might only earn 5–10% APY, but it's pure profit with minimal risk. Graduate to correlated pairs like WBTC/ETH where both assets tend to move together. If Bitcoin pumps 50%, Ethereum often pumps 40–60%, keeping your ratio relatively stable. Blue-chip volatile pairs like ETH/USDC should come only after you've experienced IL firsthand and understand the trade-off. Also, never provide liquidity for tokens you wouldn't hold independently. A rule of thumb to follow is if you wouldn't buy it outright, don't LP it. That memecoin offering 500% APY will likely go to zero, taking half your pool with it.

Monitor volume-to-TVL ratios to find the fee machines. This ratio tells you how efficiently a pool generates fees. A pool with $1 million TVL doing $1 million daily volume (1.0 ratio) means the entire pool turns over daily, generating massive fees. At 0.3% fees, that's potentially 100%+ APY. Compare this to a pool with $10 million TVL doing $100k daily volume (0.01 ratio). Same fee tier, but 100x less efficient. During volatile periods, some pools see 5–10x volume/TVL ratios. These are the pools where impermanent loss becomes easier to manage because fees dwarf any divergence loss. Check these ratios on analytics sites before entering any position.

Use wider ranges in concentrated liquidity positions. When you advance to concentrated positions in chapter 21, resist the temptation to set ultra-tight ranges chasing maximum fees. A position concentrated between $1,900 and $2,100 for ETH might earn 50x fees but will quickly go out of range, and if you rebalance to get back into range you'll be locking in impermanent loss. A wider range like $1,500–$3,000 might earn "only" 10x fees but stays active much longer, continuously earning while avoiding severe IL. You don't need the tightest range to earn excellent returns. Consistency beats intensity almost every single time.

Hedge with options or perpetuals for large positions. Advanced strategies involve buying protective options against large price movements. If you're providing $100k in ETH/USDC liquidity, buying some ETH calls protects you against ETH mooning. If ETH goes from $2k to $10k, your impermanent loss might be $20k, but your calls could profit $25k, leaving you net positive plus all fees earned. Similarly, buying puts protects you against crashes. This is complex and requires capital for premiums, but for positions over $50k, the protection can be worth it. Some professionals maintain delta-neutral positions using perpetual futures, constantly adjusting to maintain zero directional exposure while earning pure fees.

Rebalance strategically, not emotionally. If your ETH/USDC pool has shifted heavily toward USDC after an ETH pump, you have choices. You could remove liquidity and re-enter at the new ratio, locking in the impermanent loss but starting fresh. Or you could wait for mean reversion. The key is making these decisions based on analysis, not emotion. If ETH pumped on genuine adoption news, rebalancing might make sense. If it pumped on speculation, waiting for reversion might be smarter.

Remember: the goal isn't to eliminate impermanent loss entirely. That's impossible in volatile pairs. The goal is to ensure fees exceed IL by enough to generate attractive net returns. A pool suffering 10% IL but generating 50%

in fees still nets 40% returns. Focus on the total return, not individual components. Plus, remember that what you do with the fees you earn is equally important. You can dramatically enhance your returns if you use fees to build your bags or enter new positions rather than simply compounding or constantly rebalancing.

A More Advanced Borrowing Strategy

Here's an advanced strategy that neutralizes impermanent loss while keeping all the fee income, a technique that completely transforms the risk/reward equation of liquidity provision:

Instead of selling half your ETH to provide liquidity, you keep all your ETH and borrow USDC against it. Platforms like Aave, Compound, or Maker let you deposit ETH and borrow stablecoins at 50–70% loan-to-value ratios. Now you provide liquidity with borrowed funds while maintaining full ETH exposure.

Let's walk through the mechanics with real numbers. You have 10 ETH worth $20,000.

The traditional LP approach: Sell 5 ETH for $10,000 USDC, provide liquidity with 5 ETH + $10,000 USDC. If ETH doubles to $4,000, your LP position suffers impermanent loss and you miss half the gains on your ETH.

The borrowing approach: Keep all 10 ETH. Deposit them in Aave as collateral. Borrow $10,000 USDC at a max 50% LTV (we recommend a much safer buffer to avoid liquidation, but we'll use 50% for easy math in this example). Provide liquidity with your borrowed $10,000 USDC. Now, if ETH doubles, your collateral (10 ETH) is worth $40,000, capturing the full gain. Your LP position still experiences impermanent loss, but who cares? You own 10 ETH that doubled, not 5.

The mathematics work because borrowing costs (typically 3–10% APY on stablecoins) are often much lower than LP fees (20–100% APY on volatile pairs). If you're earning 50% APY from fees but paying 5% APY to borrow, you're netting 45% yield while maintaining full ETH exposure. The impermanent loss becomes irrelevant because you never sold your ETH to begin with.

Risk management is critical with this strategy. Never borrow at maximum LTV. If you can borrow up to 75%, stop at 50% to create a liquidation buffer. Monitor your health factor constantly. If ETH drops significantly, you might need to add collateral or repay some debt to avoid liquidation. Many LPs using this strategy got liquidated in May 2021 when ETH crashed from $4,000 to $1,700 in days. Use the fees you're earning to either pay down debt or add ETH for more collateral.

The tax implications can actually improve with this approach. In many jurisdictions, borrowing isn't a taxable event, but selling ETH for USDC is. By borrowing instead of selling, you defer taxes while generating income. The interest paid on loans might even be tax-deductible depending on your situation and location.

Advanced practitioners layer multiple strategies. They might borrow USDC against ETH, provide ETH/USDC liquidity, then stake the LP tokens for additional rewards. Or borrow against multiple assets to create diversified LP positions. Some, like I just mentioned, even use the fees earned to gradually repay the loan, eventually owning the LP position outright with no debt.

The psychological benefit is enormous. Holders of traditional LPs constantly stress about impermanent loss when their preferred asset pumps. With this strategy, you're rooting for both outcomes. ETH pumps? Your collateral value explodes. ETH dumps? You're earning massive fees from panic trading. ETH goes sideways? Pure fee generation with no IL. Every scenario becomes profitable.

This strategy works best in bull markets when your collateral is appreciating. In bear markets, managing liquidation risk becomes paramount. Some liquidity providers switch strategies based on market conditions, like borrowing during bulls and using owned capital during bears. The flexibility to adapt your approach based on market conditions is what separates profitable liquidity providers from those who just chase yields blindly, and the ease of switching strategies with zero wait time is what makes DeFi so powerful.

Reframing Impermanent Loss: The Cost of Being the House

After years of providing liquidity, I've learned to see impermanent loss differently. It's not a loss; it's the cost of running a market-making business. This is why I like to call it a DeFi business. Every business has costs. Restaurants have food costs. Retailers have inventory costs. Liquidity providers have impermanent loss. The question isn't whether you'll have costs but whether your revenue will exceed them.

When someone warns you about impermanent loss, ask them if they've calculated the fee income. Ask if they understand that they're running a business, not making a traditional investment. Ask if they've considered that 50% APY with 10% impermanent loss still nets 40% returns. Most critics of liquidity provision focus obsessively on IL while ignoring the income side of the equation.

The traders using your liquidity are paying you for a service. The impermanent loss you experience is your inventory management cost. As long as fees exceed costs, you're running a profitable operation. Every ratio shift means trades happened. Every trade means fees. Every fee means income.

Your Complete Impermanent Loss Action Plan

Start with stable pairs to learn without pain. USDC/USDT has near-zero impermanent loss but still earns 5–15% APY from arbitrage trades. This is your training ground where you learn the mechanics without the stress. Track everything from day one: fees earned, position value, total returns. You can use our free portfolio tracker at DeFiBuddy.io to monitor all your positions automatically.

Graduate to correlated pairs like ETH/stETH or WBTC/cbBTC. These offer minimal impermanent loss with at least some yields. You're earning from genuine trading volume with very low divergence risk. Watch how these pairs behave during market moves. Notice how quickly arbitrageurs restore the peg when prices diverge.

Move to major pairs once you understand the dynamics. ETH/USDC might experience significant impermanent loss, but during volatile periods, the fee generation often more than compensates. Start small, maybe $1,000, and track meticulously. Calculate your net returns including both fees and IL. Most successful liquidity providers find that volatile pairs during high-volume periods are their biggest earners despite the IL.

Consider advanced strategies like borrowing against holdings to provide liquidity without sacrificing exposure. Keep your 10 ETH, borrow USDC against it, and provide liquidity with borrowed funds. Now impermanent loss doesn't matter, because you still own all your ETH. The 5% or so borrowing cost is easily covered by 50% LP yields, netting you 45% income while maintaining full upside exposure.

Most importantly, focus on total returns, not individual components. A position earning 50% in fees with 15% impermanent loss is still delivering 35% net returns. That beats any traditional investment. The obsession with avoiding IL at all costs prevents most people from earning the generous yields available in DeFi.

And finally, remember that impermanent loss is simply the cost of being the market maker. It's not something to be afraid of; it's the natural result of providing two-sided liquidity. When you accept this, you stop fearing it and start managing it. You begin to see IL as a business expense that enables much larger revenue generation.

Think about traditional market makers on Wall Street. They constantly buy assets they don't want and sell assets they do want, taking small losses on inventory management. But they make it up in volume, earning the spread on millions of trades. You're doing the exact same thing, except the blockchain handles all the complexity automatically.

The psychological shift is crucial. Instead of checking your position value obsessively and panicking about IL, you start checking your fee earnings and celebrating the volume. Bad days become relative. Sure, you might have some IL today, but you earned $50 in fees. Over a month, a quarter, a year, those fees compound into serious income.

Remember: every DEX trade happens through someone's liquidity. The billions in daily volume generate millions in daily fees. Those fees flow to liquidity providers who understand that impermanent loss is just the cost of capturing this income stream. You can be the one earning these fees, or you can be the one paying them. The choice is yours.

Master this concept, and you'll never fear impermanent loss again. You'll understand it as simply the cost of doing business in the most profitable corner of DeFi. The house always wins in the long run, and now you understand exactly how to be the house.

In the next chapter, we'll explore the velocity of money, or how to make every dollar work like ten by borrowing against appreciating assets and deploying that capital across multiple yield-generating strategies simultaneously. This is where DeFi really gets fun.

20

The Velocity of Money:
Making Crypto Work for You

The real estate investor was explaining his strategy at a conference in 2019. "I put 20% down on a rental property, the tenants pay the mortgage, I refinance to pull my capital out, then buy another property. Same money, multiple properties."

I nodded politely, thinking he was clever. Then I discovered DeFi and realized his "advanced" strategy was primitive compared to what's possible with programmable money. He could recycle his capital maybe once every six months. In DeFi, I can deploy the same capital across five protocols in five minutes, earning from all of them simultaneously, then use those yields to open new positions that generate their own yields, all while my underlying assets appreciate. It's wealth creation on steroids.

This is the secret wealthy people have always known but rarely discuss: it's not about how much money you have, it's about how fast it moves and how many times you can use it. The Rockefellers didn't get rich by letting money sit still. They made every dollar work like ten. Now, through DeFi, you have access to velocity strategies that make theirs look antiquated.

The Velocity Secret That Built Every Fortune

Before we dive into DeFi, let's understand how the wealthy have always used velocity, because once you see this pattern, you'll recognize it everywhere.

McDonald's isn't in the burger business; they're in the real estate velocity business. Ray Kroc used franchise fees to buy properties, leased them back to franchisees, used that income to secure loans for more properties, and repeated. One dollar became ten properties, each generating income.

Amazon collects payment immediately but pays suppliers 90 days later. That float gets invested, turned into infrastructure, generates returns. They're using money that isn't even theirs yet. When Jeff Bezos talks about "customer obsession," he's really talking about velocity optimization.

Warren Buffett's insurance companies collect premiums today for events that might happen years later. That float, billions that technically belong to future claimants, gets invested in stocks and companies. He's generating returns on other people's money for decades before potentially paying it back.

Every lasting fortune used velocity to scale beyond what their own capital could support. The Medicis created modern banking by lending the same gold to multiple parties through letters of credit. Carnegie dominated steel by turning capital faster than competitors. Gates pre-sold software that didn't exist, using customer money to fund development.

The Insane Math When You Add Asset Appreciation

Here's where DeFi velocity becomes absolutely mind-blowing. Not only are you using the same capital multiple times, but when that capital is appreciating assets like ETH or BTC, you're stacking appreciation on top of velocity on top of yields.

Let me show you the math that will change how you see investing forever. Start with $100,000 of ETH at $2,500 per ETH, giving you 40 ETH. You deposit it in Aave as collateral, earning 3% APY. Then you borrow $50,000 USDC against it at 8% cost and deploy that $50,000 into liquidity pools earning 60% APY.

Now watch what happens over one year if ETH doubles to $5,000. Your original 40 ETH is now worth $200,000, a $100,000 gain from appreciation alone. That's a 100% return without doing anything. But you also earned

3% lending yield on that ETH throughout the year, adding another $3,000 to your returns.

Meanwhile, your borrowed $50,000 has been working in liquidity pools earning 60% APY. That's $30,000 in LP returns. Yes, you're paying 8% to borrow that money, which costs $4,000 for the year. But your net profit from the velocity strategy is $26,000 on top of everything else.

Add it all up: you made $100,000 from ETH appreciation, $3,000 from lending yields, and $26,000 from your velocity strategy. That's $129,000 total return on your $100,000 investment, a 129% return in one year. Without velocity, you would have made just $100,000 from appreciation. The velocity strategy added an extra $29,000 to your returns.

But wait, it gets better. That $26,000 in LP profits doesn't just sit there. You deploy it into new positions earning their own yields. If you put that $26,000 into strategies earning 60% APY, that's another $15,600 annually. Those yields spawn more positions. By year end, your velocity network might be generating $4,000 monthly from yields alone.

When Bitcoin Velocity Becomes Pure Insanity

The math becomes even more insane with Bitcoin's appreciation potential. Say you have $100,000 of Bitcoin at $50,000, giving you 2 BTC. Conservative estimates put Bitcoin at $500,000 within 5-10 years. Let's be ultraconservative and say it hits $250,000 in five years.

In year one, Bitcoin appreciates to $75,000, making your 2 BTC worth $150,000. That's a $50,000 gain from appreciation. But you've also borrowed $50,000 against your BTC and deployed it at 60% APY, generating $30,000 in yields minus $4,000 in borrowing costs for a net $26,000 profit. Plus, those yields get redeployed into new positions generating another $8,000. Your total year one gain is $84,000.

Year two sees Bitcoin hit $100,000, making your 2 BTC worth $200,000, another $50,000 gain. Your original velocity positions continue generating $26,000 net, while your compounded yield positions have grown to produce $18,000 annually. Total year two gain is $94,000.

By year three, Bitcoin reaches $150,000, making your 2 BTC worth $300,000, a $100,000 gain that year. Your velocity network has expanded through yield redeployment and now generates $55,000 annually. Total year three gain is $155,000.

Year four brings Bitcoin to $200,000, making your 2 BTC worth $400,000, another $100,000 gain. Your velocity positions and compounded yields now generate $75,000 annually through the expanded network. Total year four gain is $175,000.

By year five, Bitcoin reaches $250,000, making your 2 BTC worth $500,000, a final $100,000 gain. Your velocity network now generates over $95,000 annually from dozens of positions spawned by reinvested yields. Total year five gain is $195,000.

Your five-year total return is $703,000 on a $100,000 investment, a 703% return. Without velocity, you'd have made $400,000 from Bitcoin appreciation alone. With velocity, you made an extra $303,000 and built an income system generating $95,000 annually that continues even if Bitcoin stops appreciating.

The Yield-to-Position Multiplication Effect

Here's where your brain might melt: yields creating positions that create yields that create positions, all while the underlying assets appreciate.

In month one, your $100,000 ETH position generates $2,500 in various yields across your velocity strategies. That $2,500 becomes a new position earning 60% APY.

Month two sees your original positions generate another $2,500, while your new position generates $125. That $2,625 opens another position.

By month six, you have fifteen active positions spawned entirely from yields, collectively generating $6,000 monthly.

After one year, your yield-spawned positions are generating more than your original positions. You've created a self-replicating money machine.

Meanwhile, if ETH doubles during that year, your original $100,000 is now worth $200,000. This increases your borrowing power, enabling larger velocity plays. You can now borrow $100,000 instead of $50,000, doubling your velocity income. Those larger yields spawn bigger positions. It's exponential growth in three dimensions simultaneously.

Real Examples That Prove This Works

One community member started with 32 ETH worth $50,000 when ETH was at $1,560. They lent the ETH earning 5% APY and borrowed $25,000 USDC against it, deploying that into liquidity pools. Their initial setup generated $1,200 monthly income.

After eighteen months with ETH at $4,000, their 32 ETH was worth $128,000, a 156% appreciation gain. They'd accumulated 2.4 ETH from rewards worth $9,600. Their velocity strategies had spawned a dozen separate positions through yield redeployment. Monthly income had grown to $5,500. Their total portfolio value exceeded $195,000 from a $50,000 start.

Another member started with 1 BTC worth $30,000. They used it as collateral to borrow $15,000, which they deployed across strategies earning 60% APY. Initial monthly income was $750. After two years with BTC at $65,000, they'd gained $35,000 from appreciation while never selling any Bitcoin. Their velocity network had expanded to 6 active positions generating $4,800 monthly. Total portfolio value exceeded $115,000 from the $30,000 start.

The Compound Velocity Formula

Here's the formula that builds empires: **Asset Appreciation (A)** plus **Staking Yield (Y)**, multiplied by your **Velocity Multiplier (V)**, compounded through **Yield Redeployment (R)**, and expanded over **Time (T)**, equals **Exponential Wealth (W)**.

$$W_T = \left(A \times (1 + Y \times R)\right)^T \times V^T \times W_0$$

Let's walk through real numbers assuming ETH doubles annually in bull markets, earning 5% lending yield, using a conservative 2x velocity multiplier (borrowing 50% against holdings) and redeploying 100% of yields. Over three years, the math is staggering.

Year One: Your $100,000 ETH doubles to $,000 from appreciation. You earned 5% lending yield ($5,000) on your ETH. You borrowed $50,000 against your ETH and deployed it at 40% APY (conservative DeFi yields), generating $20,000 minus $4,000 borrowing costs = $16,000 net. That $16,000 gets redeployed, earning an additional $3,200 by year end. Total value: $224,200.

Year Two: Your $224,200 base doubles from appreciation to $448,400. Lending yield on your original ETH (now worth $400,000) generates $10,000. Your velocity strategies continue: borrowing against the appreciated ETH lets you deploy $100,000 at 40% APY for $40,000 gross, minus $8,000 borrowing costs = $32,000 net. Your previous year's redeployed yields ($19,200) now generate $7,680. Total value: $498,080.

Year Three: Your $498,080 doubles from appreciation to $996,160. Lending yield generates $20,000. Velocity strategies with $200,000 borrowed capital generate $80,000 gross minus $16,000 costs = $64,000 net. Your compounded yield network from previous years now generates $35,000+. Total value exceeds $1,115,000, with a yield network generating $8,000+ monthly.

Without velocity, $100,000 becomes $800,000 through appreciation alone (doubling three times). With velocity, it becomes $1,115,000 plus an $8,000 monthly income system. That $315,000 difference, plus the ongoing income stream, is the velocity premium that the wealthy have always understood.

The key insight: each layer compounds on the others. Appreciation increases your borrowing power. Borrowing enables yield generation. Yields get redeployed into new positions. Time multiplies everything. We're not playing the addition game; we're full throttle with multiplication.

Put another way, you can think of it like the network effect we talked about earlier. Each velocity position doesn't exist in isolation. They create a network that becomes more valuable than the sum of its parts. The appreciation of your ETH increases your borrowing power. More borrowing enables more yield generation. More yields create more positions. More positions create more opportunity. It's a self-reinforcing wealth spiral.

When ETH pumps, your collateral value increases, reducing liquidation risk and allowing higher leverage for more yields. When yields are high, you accumulate more positions. When yields compress, your accumulated positions still generate income while you wait for the next opportunity.

This network becomes antifragile. Market volatility that destroys single positions strengthens velocity networks. Crashes create buying opportunities funded by yields. Pumps create profit-taking opportunities that spawn new positions.

From Idle Money to Empire Building!

If you have $50,000 in ETH sitting in a wallet, you're losing money even as ETH appreciates. That ETH could be collateral earning staking rewards while enabling borrowing that funds liquidity generating yields that spawn positions. Same ETH ownership, but 2x the returns.

Start simple by using your ETH or BTC as collateral, borrowing conservatively, and deploying into safe yields. As you gain confidence, add layers. Let yields create new positions. Build your velocity network gradually but deliberately. Remember that every dollar sitting idle is a dollar dying. Every asset not generating yield is opportunity cost. Every yield not redeployed is compound growth abandoned.

In five years, operating without velocity will seem as primitive as keeping cash under your mattress. The question isn't whether to implement velocity strategies, but how aggressive to be. Traditional finance is trying to tokenize assets for 2x velocity. We're already at 10x and accelerating. By the time they catch up to where we are today, we'll be at 20x velocity with strategies they haven't imagined.

The wealthy have always known this secret: make every dollar work like ten. They just did it slowly through banks, real estate, and businesses. You can do it at light speed through DeFi, with appreciating crypto assets as your foundation. Your ETH isn't just going to $10,000. It's going there while generating yields, enabling velocity, spawning positions, and creating income systems. That's the difference between getting rich slowly and building wealth exponentially.

Your dollars will never be lazy again. They'll be working, multiplying, appreciating, and spawning new dollars that do the same. This is how modern empires are built. The rich have always known this secret. Now you do, too!

21

Advanced DeFi:
Concentrated Liquidity and Next-Level Yield

I'll never forget the moment I discovered concentrated liquidity. I was providing full-range liquidity for ETH/USDC, earning a respectable 25% APY. Then someone showed me their Uniswap V3 position in the same pool, focused on a tight range, earning 250% APY. Same pool. Same assets. Ten times the returns.

My brain broke trying to understand how this was possible. How could focusing liquidity in a price range multiply returns by 10x? Once I understood the mechanics, I realized this wasn't a fluke or unsustainable yield farming. It was pure capital efficiency, the logical evolution of everything we've learned about being the house.

After months of testing and optimization, concentrated liquidity became my highest-returning strategy. Not through luck or timing, but through understanding how to deploy capital where it's actually needed instead of spreading it across impossible price ranges.

From Shotgun to Sniper: The Concentrated Revolution

Remember how full-range liquidity works from chapter 18? Your capital spreads from zero to infinity, ready to facilitate trades at any price. It's like being a store that stocks everything from penny candy to Lamborghinis.

Most of your inventory never sells because ETH isn't going to $1 or $1 million anytime soon.

Concentrated liquidity changes this completely. Instead of spreading your $10,000 across all prices, you focus it on a specific range where trading actually happens. If ETH is at $3,000, you might provide liquidity only between $2,700 and $3,300. Your entire $10,000 works within that range.

The math is beautifully simple. If 90% of trading happens in that 10% price range, and if you concentrate all your capital there instead of spreading it everywhere, you capture 10x more fees per dollar. Same capital, same pool, but 10x more efficient deployment.

Think about it like this. Full-range liquidity is a shotgun blast hoping to hit something. Concentrated liquidity is a sniper rifle aimed exactly where the target will be. When you're right about the range, precision pays off magnificently.

How Concentrated Positions Actually Work

When you create a concentrated position, you're essentially making a bet about where price will be. Set your range from $2,800 to $3,200 for ETH, and your liquidity exists only within those bounds. Every trade that happens within your range earns you fees. Every trade outside your range earns you nothing.

Here's where it gets interesting. Because your liquidity is concentrated, you earn a much larger share of fees when price is in your range. Instead of providing 1% of the total pool liquidity in full range, you might be providing 10% of the effective liquidity in your concentrated range. Ten times the fee share with the same capital.

But there's a catch that builds on everything we learned about impermanent loss. As price moves through your range, the AMM automatically converts your assets. Start with 50/50 ETH/USDC at $3,000. If ETH rises to your upper bound of $3,200, you'll be 100% USDC. If it falls to your lower bound of $2,800, you'll be 100% ETH.

This automatic conversion is impermanent loss on steroids within your range. But here's the key insight: if you're earning 10x the fees, you can handle more impermanent loss and still be profitable. A position earning 200% APY can absorb 50% impermanent loss and still net 150% returns. That said, with more power comes greater responsibility.

Range Selection: The Art and Science

Through managing hundreds of concentrated positions, I've learned that range selection determines everything. Too wide, and you're basically doing full range with extra steps. Too narrow, and you're constantly out of range, earning nothing and locking in permanent loss with every rebalance.

For stable pairs like USDC/USDT, go extremely narrow. These pairs trade between $0.99 and $1.01, so set your range at $0.995 to $1.005. You'll capture fees from every arbitrage trade while rarely going out of range. Some positions earn 20%+ APY on stablecoins with zero price risk.

For volatile blue-chips like ETH/USDC, I define my range using a combination of support/resistance levels and ATR (average true range) bands. ATR measures actual volatility over a period, typically 14 days. It tells you how much an asset typically moves, letting you size your range based on real market behavior rather than guessing.

Here's how ATR bands work: if ETH is at $3,000 and the ATR is $100, that means ETH typically moves $100 per day. You create bands by adding and subtracting multiples of ATR from the current price. A 1x ATR band would be $2,900 to $3,100. A 2x ATR band would be $2,800 to $3,200. These act like dynamic support and resistance levels that expand when volatility is high and contract when it's low.

This is game-changing for range selection. During quiet markets when ATR drops to $50, you can run tighter ranges like $2,925 to $3,075 for maximum capital efficiency. When volatility spikes and ATR jumps to $150, you automatically know to widen to $2,700 to $3,300 or more to avoid getting knocked out constantly. The market tells you exactly how wide your range should be.

I typically use 1.5x to 2x ATR bands for positions I want to monitor daily, and 3x-4x ATR bands for positions I want to "set and forget" for weeks. A 2x

ATR band on ETH might earn 8-10x base yields while staying in range 80% of the time. It's the sweet spot between capital efficiency and maintenance.

For trending markets, combine ATR with directional bias. If ETH is in an uptrend from $2,500 with an ATR of $100, don't set a symmetric range. Use something like $2,400 to $2,700 (skewed upward) to stay in range longer as price grinds higher. You're using ATR for width but trend analysis for positioning.

The width of your range is a direct trade-off between capital efficiency and maintenance. A 10% range might earn 5x base yields. A 5% range might earn 12x but requires constant monitoring. ATR bands give you a data-driven framework for finding your sweet spot between returns and effort, adapting automatically to market conditions rather than using arbitrary percentages.

Active Management: The Price of Multiplication

Here's what nobody tells you about concentrated liquidity: it requires active management. This isn't set-and-forget like full-range positions. When price exits your range, you're earning zero. You need to either close the position and redeploy at a new range, or wait for price to return.

This creates a fascinating dynamic. You're not just providing liquidity; you're actively predicting where liquidity will be needed. Get it right, and you may earn 10x returns. Get it wrong, and you earn nothing while missing opportunity.

The rebalancing decision is where fortunes are made or lost. Let's say price exits your range upward, meaning you're now 100% in the quote token (usually stablecoins). Do you immediately reset your range higher, potentially buying back at worse prices? Or wait for a pullback that might never come?

Through painful experience, I've developed a framework that removes emotion from these decisions. First, I follow the 24–48 hour rule: when price exits my range, I don't touch anything for at least a day. Markets are often emotionally driven in the short term, so that spike that took you out of range might reverse just as quickly. I've watched countless positions pop back into range within 48 hours after an emotional market move.

If price remains out of range after 48 hours and has moved significantly (more than 5–10% beyond my range), then I assess whether this is a fundamental shift or emotional overreaction. News-driven moves often reverse. Technical breakouts often continue. Fed announcements create temporary volatility. Understanding the "why" behind the move helps you determine whether to rebalance or wait.

When I do rebalance, I accept it as a cost of doing business. Yes, this means taking impermanent loss. But staying out of range earning nothing while liquidity is desperately needed elsewhere is worse than accepting the loss and getting back to earning. The fees from being in the right range for a week can easily overcome the loss from one rebalancing.

Gas costs on Layer 2s make this strategy viable. On Arbitrum or Base, rebalancing costs $1–2 or less, making active management profitable even for smaller positions. You can rebalance a $500 position without fees destroying your returns.

The key is having rules before emotions hit. Write down your rebalancing criteria when you're calm. Maybe it's 48 hours out of range. Maybe it's 10% price movement. Maybe it's based on volume drying up in your range. Whatever your rules, follow them mechanically. The market doesn't care about your feelings, and neither should your rebalancing strategy.

Leveraged Yield Farming: Velocity on Steroids (*Not for Everyone)

Remember velocity from chapter 20? Now add leverage to concentrated positions for truly insane returns. This is advanced and risky, as leverage usually is, but the math is mind-blowing.

Start with $10,000. Use it as collateral to borrow $5,000. Deploy that $15,000 into a concentrated position earning 200% APY. Your $10,000 is now earning returns on $15,000, effectively 300% APY. But we're not done.

Take the LP tokens from your concentrated position and use them as collateral elsewhere. Borrow another $7,500 against them. Deploy that into another concentrated position. Now your original $10,000 is controlling $22,500 in concentrated positions.

If both positions earn 200% APY, you're generating $45,000 annually from your $10,000. Subtract borrowing costs of maybe $3,000, and you're netting $42,000 on $10,000. That's 420% APY through leveraged concentrated liquidity.

Note: The risks here are massive. Liquidation cascades, impermanent loss, rebalancing costs, smart contract risks, all multiplied by leverage. This isn't for beginners or the faint-hearted. But for those who understand the risks and manage them properly, the returns are life-changing. I always suggest that everyone considering playing this game should first take $100 and leverage it multiple times, just to see how quickly you can make money and just how fast you can lose it all.

The Psychology of Active Management

Concentrated liquidity transforms you from passive provider to active manager, and this psychological shift is harder than the technical learning. You're no longer just earning fees; you're making constant decisions that directly impact returns. Every hour price stays in your range, you're earning 10x what full-range providers make. Every hour outside your range, you're earning zero while watching others profit.

The temptation to overtrade becomes your biggest enemy. Price moves 1% outside your range, and your brain screams to rebalance immediately. But each rebalancing has real costs: gas fees, slippage, and locked-in impermanent loss. Through painful experience, I've learned that oftentimes the best decision is to do nothing. Markets are emotional in the short term but mathematical in the long term. That spike that took you out of range often reverses within 48 hours.

Again, this is why I follow the 24–48 hour rule religiously. When price exits my range, I don't touch anything for at least a day. This simple rule has saved me thousands in unnecessary rebalancing costs. During that waiting period, I assess whether a move would be emotional or fundamental. Fed announcement? Usually reverses. Technical breakout with volume? Probably continues. News-driven spike with no follow-through? Almost always returns to range.

When price is out of your range, FOMO will test your discipline constantly. Watching volume explode while your position earns nothing feels like being robbed in broad daylight. Your competitors are earning 10x fees from the volatility you're missing. But chasing price by constantly rebalancing is exactly how you turn a profitable strategy into a loss-making hamster wheel. The fees you miss during one day out of range are nothing compared to the losses from panic-rebalancing at the worst possible prices.

When you nail a range perfectly, the satisfaction is genuinely addictive. I once set an ETH range that stayed active for six weeks during a consolidation, earning 15x normal yields while never touching it. It felt like I'd achieved market mastery. But that overconfidence led me to set progressively tighter ranges, triggering more rebalancing, more costs, and eventual losses. The market humbles everyone who thinks they've figured it out.

The key is developing mechanical rules that override emotions. My framework: if price stays out of range for 48 hours *and* has moved more than 10% beyond my bounds, I rebalance. If volume in my range drops below 25% of normal for three days, I reassess. If a major event is coming (Fed meetings, upgrades, earnings), I widen ranges preemptively. These rules remove emotion from decisions that would otherwise be driven by fear and greed.

Starting Your Concentrated Liquidity Journey

Start your concentrated journey with wide ranges on major pairs. ETH/USDC with 20% ranges ($2,700–$3,300 when ETH is at $3,000) is perfect for learning. You'll earn 3–4x full-range yields while rarely needing to rebalance. This gives you time to understand the mechanics without the stress of constant management. Track everything: fees earned, time in range, gas costs, rebalancing frequency. This data becomes your education.

Use ATR bands to size your ranges scientifically rather than guessing. If ETH's 14-day ATR is $100, a 2x ATR band ($2,800–$3,200) historically captures about 80% of price action. This removes the guesswork and gives you a data-driven framework that adapts to market conditions. During low volatility, ATR might drop to $50, letting you tighten to $2,925–$3,075 for higher yields. During high volatility, ATR might spike to $150, telling you to widen to $2,700–$3,300 to avoid constant rebalancing.

Progress to tighter ranges as you gain experience and confidence. Move from 20% to 15% to 10% ranges gradually, but only after mastering each level. Each tightening multiplies returns but exponentially increases management requirements. A 2% range might earn 12x base yields but requires hourly monitoring and daily rebalancing. A 20% range might earn "only" 3x but lets you sleep peacefully for weeks. Find your personal balance between returns and lifestyle.

Layer 2s make this entire strategy accessible to everyone. On Arbitrum or Base, rebalancing costs $1–2 instead of $100-200. This means you can profitably manage a $500 position with tight ranges, something impossible on mainnet. You can rebalance weekly without fees destroying returns. You can experiment with different strategies without risking significant capital. The democratization of concentrated liquidity is happening on L2s.

And finally, just remember that concentrated liquidity isn't magic money. It's capital efficiency maximization. You're not creating yields from nothing; you're focusing capital exactly where it's needed and being rewarded accordingly. The 10x returns are real but require 10x more attention than full-range positions. You're trading simplicity for returns.

The difference is worth the extra effort. A $10,000 position in a full-range pool might earn $2,000 annually. Shift that same $10,000 into a well-managed concentrated position, and during volatile markets it can generate **5–10x the fees**. We've seen stretches where positions earned $100 daily on $10K. Same assets, same pool, just smarter deployment. Once you experience that kind of efficiency, it's hard to go back to full-range.

Welcome to the next level of liquidity provision. Remember, start small, go slow, and, just as importantly, have fun with it!

22

The Future of DeFi:
Where the Financial Revolution Is Headed

The transaction would have cost me $147 on Ethereum mainnet. I was trying to swap $500 worth of tokens, and the gas fee was almost 30% of my trade. Then someone told me about Layer 2 solutions. Same trade, same tokens, same outcome. Cost: $0.43.

That 340x reduction wasn't just a technical improvement. It was the unlock that will make everything we dream about in DeFi actually possible. But first, let me explain what gas fees actually are and why Layer 2s matter so much for the future.

Understanding Gas Fees and Layer 2 Solutions

Gas fees are what you pay for computation on Ethereum. Every transaction requires processing power from thousands of nodes worldwide. When you swap tokens or provide liquidity, you're paying for that computational work. Network activity determines the price, so higher demand means higher fees.

This economic model, while ensuring network security, led to the development of Layer 2 solutions. These Layer 2s process transactions off the main chain and settle them in batches, achieving the same security with 99% lower costs. Think of it like carpooling instead of everyone driving separately. Hundreds of transactions share one Ethereum transaction, splitting the cost.

On Arbitrum, Base, or Optimism, that swap can now cost $0.50 or less. Providing liquidity costs $1 instead of potential mainnet fees of $20–50. Rebalancing positions costs $1 instead of higher mainnet costs. This isn't a different blockchain; it's still Ethereum, just more efficient. Today, most DeFi users operate on Layer 2s where experiments with $100 cost pennies in fees, not dollars. Layer 2s have made everything we've covered in this book practical for everyone, not just whales.

Now let's talk about what will become possible as this technology evolves. Layer 2s today are just the foundation for something much bigger. We'll be moving fast through these ideas, but this is the stuff that genuinely excites me about where we're headed. As investors and builders, we're so early it's almost absurd. The opportunities over the next decade aren't just numerous; they're essentially unlimited for those who position themselves now.

The Scaling Revolution Coming Next

Layer 2s are winning the scaling war, but we're just getting started. The next wave of improvements will reduce costs another 10–100x. When transactions that cost $0.10 today drop to $0.001, blockchain will become cheaper than Visa, faster than SWIFT, and more accessible than any bank.

The user experience revolution will eliminate every remaining friction point. Account abstraction will mean no more seed phrases, no more buying ETH for gas, no more complex bridging. Wallets will become as simple as Venmo but with the power of the entire DeFi ecosystem behind them. Smart wallets will recover from lost keys, batch transactions automatically, and pay fees in any token.

Real-world assets will flood onto chains at scale. Tokenized treasuries are just the beginning. When stocks, bonds, real estate, and commodities all become tradeable 24/7 with instant settlement, traditional markets will seem archaic. Imagine buying $10 of Apple stock at 3 a.m. on Sunday for $0.001 in fees and having it earning yield in DeFi minutes later.

Major banks and fintechs will integrate Layer 2 access directly into their apps. Buying USDC or ETH will become as easy as using PayPal. Your grandma won't know she's using blockchain; she'll just know sending money is instant and nearly free.

The Coming Professionalization Wave

The wild west days of DeFi are numbered. Professional tools will emerge that make yield farming as simple as index fund investing. We're seeing early versions with auto-compounders, but the future will bring AI-powered strategies that optimize across protocols automatically.

Risk management will become invisible and automatic. Future protocols will hedge impermanent loss by default. Vaults will dynamically adjust leverage based on market conditions without user intervention. Insurance will pay out instantly based on smart contract conditions, no claims process needed. The sharp edges that cut early adopters will be completely smoothed away.

A new profession will emerge: DeFi strategists who manage complex positions for others. Just like most people don't pick individual stocks but invest in index funds, most users won't manage individual LP positions but invest in professionally managed vaults. The returns will stay high, but the complexity will disappear entirely.

The Creator Economy Revolution Ahead

Social media is just beginning to move to blockchain with experiments like Friend.tech and Lens Protocol. When posting costs drop to fractions of a penny everywhere, the entire creator economy will transform. Every like will become a potential micropayment. Every share will distribute value automatically. Content will generate direct revenue for creators without platforms extracting their current massive cuts.

In the future, your social graph will be portable and valuable. Followers won't be locked to Twitter or Instagram; they'll be recorded on chain, following you across any platform. You'll build an audience once and own it forever. Platforms will compete to serve creators rather than creators begging platforms for reach.

Creator tokens will let audiences become investors in their favorite artists' success. Support someone early, own shares in their future. As they grow, early supporters benefit. It will be like buying equity in your favorite band before they get famous, except liquid and tradeable 24/7.

When micropayments become frictionless, content economics will flip entirely. Readers will pay $0.001 per article, viewers $0.01 per video, fans $0.10 for premium content. Ads will become obsolete. Data harvesting will end. The internet's business model will shift from surveillance capitalism to direct value exchange.

The Intelligent DeFi Era Approaching

AI integration will make DeFi truly intelligent. Future protocols will automatically adjust parameters for optimal performance. They'll identify and fix vulnerabilities before exploits can happen. They'll create new financial products based on observed user needs. Everyone will have a personal AI treasury manager optimizing wealth 24/7 across every protocol.

Smart contracts will become self-improving systems. They'll learn from every transaction, optimize their own gas usage, and upgrade themselves through governance. DeFi protocols will evolve like living organisms, getting stronger through use rather than degrading. The system will become increasingly robust through constant adaptation.

Cross-chain interoperability will eventually dissolve all borders between blockchains. Capital will flow seamlessly to wherever yield is highest. Arbitrage bots will ensure price consistency across every venue instantly. The distinction between Ethereum, Solana, and other chains will become irrelevant to users.

Personal DeFi management will become completely automated. AI agents will rebalance positions, harvest yields, compound returns, and optimize taxes without human intervention. They'll negotiate better rates, find arbitrage opportunities, and protect against risks. Having an AI wealth manager will become as common as having email.

A Whole New Wold Is Emerging

DAOs (decentralized autonomous organizations) will evolve from today's Discord channels into tomorrow's digital nation-states. These communities will have their own treasuries, currencies, and complete economic systems. People will choose the digital jurisdiction that aligns with their values. Geographic borders will matter less than digital affiliations.

Work will become completely fluid. Payments will stream per second. Switching between gigs will be instant. Reputation and skills will be portable across every platform. Two-week pay cycles will seem as old-school as mailing checks. Value transfer will become as simple as sending a message.

The unbanked will leapfrog traditional finance entirely. When the infrastructure is complete, a farmer in Nigeria will access the same yields as a hedge fund in Manhattan. A programmer in Vietnam will receive the same instant payments as one in Silicon Valley. Geography will become completely irrelevant to economic opportunity.

Traditional financial services will migrate on chain. Insurance claims will process automatically via smart contracts. Mortgages will be transparent and instant. Business loans will be collateralized and immediate. The inefficiencies that make traditional finance expensive will disappear.

Maximum Money Velocity in the Future

Here's where the future gets truly wild. Money will work everywhere simultaneously. The same assets will earn yield in multiple protocols at once. Your ETH will serve as collateral for a loan, that loan will provide liquidity, that liquidity will earn fees, those fees will auto compound into new positions. Every dollar will work like ten dollars.

This isn't fantasy; early versions are being built now. Future protocols will compose together in ways that multiply capital efficiency beyond current imagination. Your LP tokens will become collateral. Your collateral will earn yield. Your yield will spawn new positions automatically. Money velocity will accelerate until idle capital becomes extinct.

Synthetic assets will let anyone create any financial product instantly. Want exposure to Brazilian rainfall affecting coffee futures correlated with Bitcoin prices? Someone will create that market. The entire possibility space of finance will become accessible to everyone, not just institutions.

When costs drop low enough, every interaction can become financial. Like a post? It could trigger a micropayment. Read an article? Stream payments in real time. Use any service? Pay exactly for what you use, per second. The friction of payment will disappear entirely. Money will flow as easily as information.

Your Role in Building Tomorrow

This future isn't that far away, either. It's being built right now by people who understand that the old system is broken beyond repair. Every liquidity position you provide today, every yield strategy you execute, every protocol you use strengthens the infrastructure of tomorrow.

The builders and early users today will become the titans tomorrow. Those providing liquidity now are establishing positions in what will become the world's financial infrastructure. Those experimenting with new protocols are learning skills that will be invaluable. Those accumulating governance tokens are buying votes in tomorrow's digital nations.

Traditional finance is trying to adapt, but it thinks incrementally while crypto builds exponentially. By the time banks offer 5% savings accounts, DeFi will offer 20% with better security. By the time they enable instant transfers, we'll have streaming money. They're optimizing horses while we're building rockets.

The Choice Before You

We stand at the inflection point between two potential futures. One where financial intermediaries continue extracting value from every transaction, where geographic boundaries determine opportunity, where the wealthy get wealthier through exclusive access. The other where finance becomes a protocol anyone can access, where geography is irrelevant, where wealth compounds for everyone equally.

The technical foundations are being laid now. The infrastructure is emerging. The network effects are beginning to compound. What remains is adoption, education, and building the bridges for the next billion users. This isn't about cryptocurrency anymore. It's literally about restructuring civilization's operating system.

Your grandchildren won't believe you when you tell them banks used to take three days to transfer money. That credit cards charged 20% interest while savings paid 0.05%. That sending money internationally cost $50 and took a week. They'll look at traditional finance the way we look at sending telegrams.

The future of DeFi isn't some distant dream. It's being built in real time, block by block, innovation by innovation. The only question is whether you'll help build it or watch others create the greatest wealth transfer in human history.

Part V:

The Investor Mindset

23

Finding Your Why:
The Inner Game of Wealth

I'm standing on the oil rig platform working a night shift at 3 a.m., northern Alberta, −40°, watching my breath freeze in the air, and I understand why people give up. Not planning anything, just understanding the despair. Another fourteen-hour shift ahead. Another two weeks before I can go home. Another year of this, and I'll have saved maybe $30,000 after taxes. Another decade, and I'll have what? A broken body and a savings account that inflation destroyed?

That moment on the platform wasn't rock bottom. Rock bottom would have been easier because it forces change. This was worse: the slow suffocation of a life that looked successful from the outside but felt empty from the inside. Good money. Respectable job. The approval of everyone who mattered. And complete, soul-crushing meaninglessness.

For years, I'd been chasing money, and the more I chased, the deeper I sank into depression. The money never filled the void. It just paid for distractions from it. Always felt like three steps forward, two steps back. The harder I chased, the farther away real wealth seemed.

Your "why" for building wealth can't be just money. If it's just money, you'll quit when business gets hard. You'll panic during market downturns. You'll abandon your strategy the moment it gets difficult. Money alone isn't enough motivation to endure the volatility, the learning curve, the failures, the judgment from others who don't understand what you're building.

The Moment Everything Changed

Six months after that night on the platform, I was sitting in a Tim Hortons in Fort McMurray, finally understanding what I'd been missing. I'd been studying successful people, and I discovered a pattern: they built wealth through entrepreneurship, investing, or both. Never just through trading time for money. They understood the difference between working for income and investment income, between being an employee and being an owner.

I remember scrolling through article after article about compound interest, passive income, and building assets instead of just earning wages. Stories of people who came from nothing and completely changed their lives. Regular people with regular jobs who learned to make their money work for them. People just like me, from small towns, without connections, without trust funds. If they could do it, so could I.

That's when my real "why" crystallized. This wasn't about getting rich or buying fancy things. It was about freedom. Freedom from being one injury away from bankruptcy. Freedom from mandatory overtime that stole my life. Freedom to wake up without an alarm. But deeper than that, it was about growth, about becoming someone who could create value instead of just trading time for money. It was about building something that would compound while I slept instead of deteriorating, the way my body was on those rigs.

My why became my fuel. Every investment book I devoured brought me closer to freedom. Every business idea I explored was a potential escape route. Every dollar saved and invested was a small rebellion against a system designed to keep me on that platform forever.

Once I found my why, everything accelerated. The same amount of effort that produced mediocre results when chasing paychecks produced extraordinary results when building toward freedom. My business gained traction. My investment portfolio grew. My content resonated with others facing similar struggles.

My why pulled me through every failure. When investments went south, when businesses struggled, when everyone thought I'd lost my mind for leaving stable employment, my why kept me going. The money followed naturally once I stopped chasing it and started pursuing my purpose.

Why Most People Fail: The Weak Foundation Problem

Most people enter investing or entrepreneurship with a weak why: "I want to get rich." This fails because it's external, not internal. It's about having more, not *becoming* more. It's about the destination, not the journey. And when the journey is all you have for years before reaching any destination, this shallow motivation crumbles at the first real challenge.

When your why is just money, every market dip becomes an existential crisis. A 20% portfolio drop makes you question everything. Every business setback becomes evidence you made a mistake. Every competitor who seems to be doing better triggers crushing self-doubt. Every failure becomes a reason to quit and return to the "safety" of employment.

The successful people, the ones who build lasting wealth over decades, have whys that transcend market movements. They're building systems that generate income without employment, creating machines that print money while they sleep. They're establishing generational wealth that breaks the poverty cycles their families have been trapped in for generations. They're constructing financial sovereignty that can't be taken away by corporate downsizing, economic recessions, or political changes. Their why is so much bigger than next month's profit that temporary losses barely register as setbacks.

I've watched hundreds of people start investing or launch businesses. The ones still standing after five years all have something in common: their why was never just about money. Money was the tool, not the goal. The goal was freedom, impact, legacy, proof of capability, breaking generational patterns, or building something meaningful. Those with money as their only motivation quit within the first year, usually at the first significant loss or challenge.

The Freedom Framework: Time Is the Only Real Wealth

There are two frameworks for thinking about wealth. Most people operate in the money framework, measuring success by net worth and bank balances.

This framework keeps you trapped forever because there's always someone with more money.

The freedom framework measures something completely different: time. The equation for financial freedom is devastatingly simple: when your passive income exceeds your expenses, you're free. That's it. Not when you have a million dollars. Not when you retire at 65. The moment your investments, businesses, and assets generate more monthly income than you spend, you own your time completely.

You could have $2 million in home equity and still need to wake up Monday morning for work you hate. But if you have $8,000 in monthly passive income and $6,000 in expenses, you're wealthier than the millionaire who still trades time for money.

Let me be clear about what this freedom means. It's not about sitting on a beach until you die of boredom. Real freedom is about doing something worth dying for every single day. Creating things that matter. Building businesses that solve problems. Helping others escape their own traps. When you don't need to work for money, you can finally do your real work. The work that uses your unique talents and makes you come alive.

The first $10,000 in monthly passive income is worth more than the next $100,000 because it buys you complete sovereignty over your existence. You've crossed the threshold from needing to work to choosing to work. Most people could achieve complete time freedom with $8,000 to $15,000 in monthly passive income, yet they spend forty years accumulating net worth they can't access while remaining slaves to their schedules.

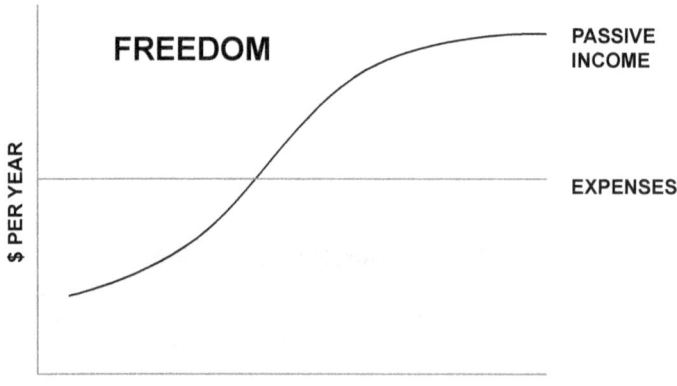

When your passive income exceeds your expenses, you're financially free.

Building Something Bigger: The Evolution of Purpose

My why evolved through stages (and continues to evolve), and yours will, too. First it was purely wanting to escape the rigs. Then material desires, like the fancy car I'd dreamed about. Then experiences—travel, restaurants, hotels. But each achievement felt hollow after the initial excitement wore off.

That's when I discovered what actually mattered to me: building things, creating community, and deepening my relationship with God. The current financial system is designed to keep people running full speed on the hamster wheel, never giving them time or space to deepen their spirituality or their relationship with God, whatever that looks like for them. We're taught to rely on and trust everything and everyone outside of ourselves, to seek validation from external authorities rather than developing our inner wisdom and connection to something greater.

When you're working 60-hour weeks just to survive, when you're constantly stressed about bills, when your entire existence revolves around the next paycheck, there's no space for spiritual growth. You can't hear your inner voice over the noise of survival. You can't explore deeper questions when every ounce of energy goes toward staying on the treadmill. The system wants it this way. Exhausted people don't question. Desperate people don't seek meaning. Busy people don't develop the spiritual foundation that might lead them to reject the whole game.

For me, financial freedom isn't just about money or time; it's about creating space for what matters most. For me, that meant space to pray and connect without rushing, to meditate without checking the clock, to study spiritual texts without exhaustion clouding my mind. It meant having the energy and presence to actually listen for guidance rather than just asking for help with my endless problems.

This spiritual dimension gave my work deeper purpose. I wanted to scale a real business. I wanted not just to make money but to build something that aligned with my values and created space for others to find their own spiritual path. And that inner voice led me to launch CryptoLabs Research.

When I started CryptoLabs, I wasn't thinking about money at all. I was absolutely obsessed with the space, but not just the technology. I saw it as a tool for liberation that could give people back their time to pursue what truly matters. I posted daily videos that got maybe 5 views. Five. My friends thought I was wasting my time. But it didn't matter because I wasn't doing it for views or validation. I was doing it because I genuinely believed this information could free people from the slavery that prevents them from discovering their own purpose and spiritual connection.

That's when my why transformed into its current form. It's not about my freedom anymore; it's about systemic change. We're democratizing financial knowledge that was previously gatekept by wealth managers and institutions. The traditional financial system thrives on complexity and exclusion. They want you dependent, not educated.

This obsession drove me to write the book you're reading right now. Every chapter represents knowledge that someone doesn't want you to have. Getting this book into your hands gives me more fulfillment than any monetary success. Right now, as you read these words, you're gaining knowledge that could change your entire financial trajectory.

When your why includes others, it becomes unstoppable. You can't quit, because people are counting on you. The exhaustion of building becomes energizing when you know it matters beyond yourself.

This evolution from escape to materialism to experience to purpose to service is natural. Don't judge yourself if you're still in the "I want a Lamborghini" phase. That's valid. But know that your why will evolve beyond just that. I'm a huge car guy. I have a Lamborghini myself, and I genuinely love driving it. The engineering, the sound, the pure joy of acceleration. But it's not my purpose for existing. It's a reward, a toy, a celebration of success, but not the reason I wake up every morning. In fact, after an hour she gets boring.

What won't get boring is building something meaningful, creating value for others, and using your unique talents to solve real problems. The Lamborghini is fun for an hour or two here and there. But building something that changes lives is fulfilling every single day. One is pleasure; the other is purpose. You can have both, but only one will sustain you through the difficult times.

The car didn't solve any deep need. It just made success more enjoyable. The real satisfaction comes from the work it took and who I became in the process, not the car itself. When you understand this distinction, you can enjoy material success without being enslaved by it. You can appreciate nice things without needing them for validation. You can drive a Lamborghini on the weekend and build something world-changing during the week.

Finding and Articulating Your True Why

To find your real why, you need to dig deeper than your surface desires. Answer these questions with brutal honesty:

- What would you do if money wasn't a constraint? Not fantasies about yachts, but how would you actually spend your days after the novelty wore off?
- What childhood passions made you lose track of time? Your original why is often buried in what lit you up before the world told you who to be.
- What makes you angry about the current system? Properly channeled anger becomes rocket fuel for transformation.
- What breaks your heart to imagine leaving unsolved? If you died tomorrow, what problem would hurt most to leave untouched?
- Who are you willing to suffer for? What cause, mission, or group would make hardship worth enduring?
- Who would you become with financial freedom? Not what you'd have, but who you'd be and how you'd show up.
- What gives you the most energy and flow? Energy is your compass pointing toward purpose.
- What legacy do you want to leave? Will you be remembered for accumulation or for impact?
- If your why is freedom, define it specifically. Freedom to wake without alarms? Travel? Create? Home-school? Specificity creates power.
- What identity must you embody to live this why? What standards and habits must you adopt to align actions with vision?
- What does your future self look like living this why? Write your ideal day ten years from now—who you're with, what you're creating, how you wake up feeling.

What small action can you take today? A true why pulls you into immediate action, even small steps.

Important: Your why will evolve as you grow. As you achieve certain goals, your perspectives and desires will shift. You're growing; that's a good thing. My why was once to simply "have $100,000 in the bank." That seemed impossible from the oil rigs, but it fueled me every single day for 2 years. Once I achieved it, my why became "never work for anyone again." Then "build a million-dollar business." Then "help others escape wage slavery."

Now part of my why is to sponsor 1,000 families in impoverished countries and regions who can't afford food, clothes, or education. We're providing support to families in Africa, Southeast Asia, and Latin America, covering their basic needs so their children can go to school instead of working. And each and every family we sponsor is another crack in the wall of an outdated system that needs to fall.

Each evolution was built on the last. The money I was desperate for became the tool to buy freedom. The freedom I achieved became the platform to build from. The business I built became the vehicle to serve others. The service to others became a mission to change systems.

Do your best with where you're at right now. Be brutally honest about what actually motivates you today, not what you think should motivate you. If your current why is "buy a house" or "pay off debt" or "prove my ex wrong", then just own it. That's your starting point. It will evolve into something bigger as you grow, but you need to start with what's real for you now, not some noble-sounding purpose you don't actually feel. The key is having a why that's powerful enough to pull you through the challenges ahead. It doesn't need to be world-changing at first. It just needs to be yours, and it needs to be true.

Your Why Starts Now, Not Someday

Finding your why isn't a philosophical exercise you do once and forget. It's the foundation of everything that follows. Without a powerful why, all the technical knowledge about investing and business is useless. You'll know what to do but lack the conviction to do it. You'll understand the strategies but abandon them during the first real challenge.

Your why is your north star during the journey to financial freedom. When markets crash 50%, return to your why. When a business fails after years of effort, return to your why. When everyone doubts you, return to your why. When complexity overwhelms, return to your why. When success comes and you're tempted to coast, return to your why to remember what comes next.

The path from wage slavery to financial sovereignty is possible. Millions have walked it before you. The knowledge you're seeking is available in books, courses, and content. The opportunity is here, perhaps more so than ever with technology democratizing access to markets and customers globally.

But without a powerful why, you'll never complete the journey. You'll start strong, hit the first real obstacle, and quit like 95% of people do. With a powerful why, nothing can stop you. Not market crashes, not business failures, not social pressure, not self-doubt. Your why becomes bigger than your fear, stronger than your comfort zone, more important than others' opinions.

What's your why? What vision of your life is so compelling that you'll do whatever it takes to achieve it? What future is worth the price of temporary discomfort, social isolation, and constant uncertainty? Find that why, commit to it completely, and you've taken the first real step toward freedom. The technical knowledge comes easily once the emotional foundation is solid. The strategies work when you have the conviction to execute them through volatility. Find your why. Fuel it. And let it pull you toward the freedom you deserve.

24

Why Everything Gets Worse
Before It Gets Better

I was sitting in a basement suite that cost $500 a month, eating ramen for the third day straight. I'd sold my car and was now riding a pedal bike instead. Two years earlier, I'd owned a condo and driven a brand new Jeep. By any conventional measure, I was going backwards.

My friends thought I'd lost my mind. Here I was, working eighteen-hour days on a business that had generated exactly zero dollars in profit over two years. I'd gone from making $100,000 on the rigs to making nothing. From living in my own place to renting a basement. From driving a new car to pedaling through rain.

"Just go back to the rigs," everyone said. "At least you had money."

But I knew something they didn't. I was in the dip of a J-curve, and J-curves are a necessary part of the journey to success. More importantly, I'd finally learned that playing small in this economy isn't just ineffective, it's financial suicide. You either bet big on yourself or accept a lifetime of mediocrity.

Two years later, that business made its first $100,000. The next business cleared half a million. The one after that broke a million. Today, I generate multi-millions annually. The J-curve that looked like failure from the outside was actually the foundation of everything.

Once You See It, You Can't Unsee It

The J-curve isn't just an investment concept or business principle. It's the fundamental pattern of how transformation works in the universe. Once you understand this, you stop seeing temporary setbacks as failures and start seeing them as necessary precursors to breakthroughs. They may even excite you rather than beat you down.

Every meaningful transformation in your life followed this pattern. Learning to walk meant falling hundreds of times first. Learning to read meant struggling with letters that made no sense. Your first relationship probably crashed and burned before you learned how to love properly.

But here's what most people get wrong: they try to navigate J-curves with half-measures. They start a business but keep their day job "just in case." They invest a few hours when success requires 10,000 hours. They dedicate weekends when victory demands every waking moment. In today's economy, with inflation destroying savings and wages that never keep up, playing it safe is the riskiest thing you can do.

When you finally accept this truth, something profound shifts in your psychology. You stop running from difficulty and start running toward it, because you understand that difficulty is just transformation in disguise. The worse something looks initially, the better it can become if you have the courage to *persist through the dip*.

The Reality of Transformation

When any system transitions from one state to a higher state, it must first pass through chaos. Think about water becoming steam. At 99° Celsius, water is still liquid. Add more energy, and something strange happens. The temperature stops rising. All that additional energy goes into breaking molecular bonds, transforming the water's state. To an observer, it looks like nothing's happening. The energy seems wasted. But at the moment of transformation, all that stored energy releases, and water becomes steam with vastly more power and possibility.

Your business, investments, and personal growth follow identical physics. The energy you put in during the dip isn't disappearing. It's breaking old patterns and building new capabilities. The lack of visible progress isn't failure; it's transformation happening at a structural level that you can't yet see.

This understanding changed everything for me. When my business wasn't making money, I wasn't failing; I was storing energy for transformation. When my crypto investments crashed, they weren't dying; they were consolidating for the next leap. Doubling down when everyone else sold at a loss and ran for the hills was building future wealth.

The J-curve isn't something that happens to you. It's something that happens for you. It's life's way of ensuring that only those with genuine commitment reach the next level. It's the gym where you build your strength and character. It's a filter that keeps tourists out and lets those who are serious about success through.

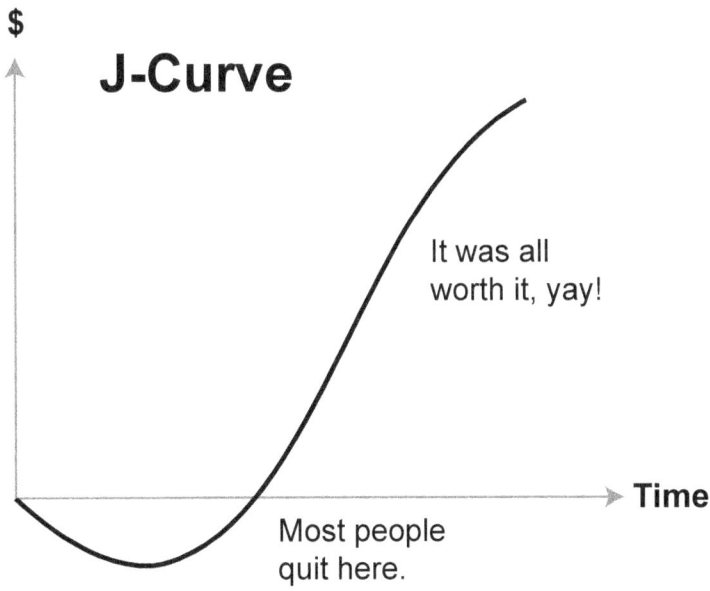

Why Playing Small Is Playing to Lose

The brutal truth about today's economy: the middle class is being systematically destroyed. Inflation eats 7–10% of your savings annually. Wages haven't kept up with costs for decades. The traditional path—get a job, save money, retire at 65—is mathematically impossible for most people.

In this environment, small bets don't just fail to win; they guarantee you lose. Saving $100 a month? Inflation destroys it. Starting a side hustle you work on weekends? It'll never reach escape velocity. Investing $1,000 when you have $50,000 sitting in savings? You're choosing poverty through timidity.

When I left the rigs, I didn't keep a backup plan. I didn't maintain a safety net. I sold everything, burned the boats, and went all in on transformation. Was it scary? Absolutely. Was it risky? On paper, yes. But was it riskier than staying on the rigs, trading my body for money that inflation would destroy anyway? Not even close.

The economy has split into two groups: those who bet big on themselves and win, and those who play it safe and lose slowly. There's no middle ground anymore. You're either growing exponentially or declining gradually. You're either building assets that outpace inflation or watching your purchasing power evaporate.

My Business J-Curve: The "All-In" Advantage

The decision to leave the rigs wasn't brave; it was desperate. I was depressed, I hated my life, and I felt frustrated, stuck, and angry at everything. But desperation plus commitment equals transformation.

My first business was personal training, chosen not from passion but because it was what I knew. I was fit from the rigs and figured that was enough. It wasn't. For two years I bled money, dignity, and confidence. The Jeep went first, sold to cover expenses. Then the apartment, leading to that $500 basement suite.

But here's what gave me an edge: I had no backup plan. While my competitors were doing personal training as a side hustle, keeping their comfortable jobs, I was eighteen hours deep every single day. While they were reading one business book a month, I was consuming everything—books, courses, podcasts, YouTube videos—like my life depended on it, because it did.

The psychological toll was brutal. Buddies from the rigs would check in, and their pity was obvious. My family stopped asking how the business was going. Friends stopped inviting me out because they knew I couldn't afford it. I was twenty-six years old, living like a broke college student, with nothing to show for two years of eighteen-hour days.

But beneath the surface, invisible assets were accumulating: Knowledge that couldn't be taught, only earned. Skills that couldn't be bought, only built. Resilience that couldn't be gifted, only forged through repetition. The J-curve was transforming me from someone who worked for money into someone who could create money from nothing.

When success finally came, it came fast. Month twenty-three brought the first $1,000 profit. Month twenty-four: $2,000. Month thirty: $10,000. By year three, I'd saved $100,000. Not revenue. Saved. The business was profitable and growing. And each business after was easier to start, grew quicker, was easier to scale, and was more profitable than the last. The momentum compounded, and each success taught lessons that accelerated the next venture. The network grew stronger. The skills sharpened. The confidence solidified. What took three years for the first business took six months for the second, three months for the third. The pattern recognition from repeated success became its own advantage.

My competitors who kept their safety nets? They're still doing personal training as a side hustle. Still working their jobs. Still playing small. The J-curve rewards those who commit completely and punishes those who hedge their bets.

The Crypto J-Curve Advantage

In crypto, understanding J-curves while being willing to bet big is worth more than any technical analysis. While others panic with their $1,000 positions during dips, you accumulate with conviction using real capital. This is where everything we've discussed converges into actionable wealth-building.

Bitcoin has had multiple J-curves, and each one followed the pattern we explored in chapter 11. The 2011 crash from $32 to $2 was a 94% drawdown. The 2013 to 2015 bear saw prices fall from $1,163 to $152, an 87% collapse. The 2017 to 2018 crash took Bitcoin from $20,000 to $3,200, an 84% decline. The 2021 to 2022 collapse brought it from $69,000 to $15,500, a 78% drawdown.

Each felt like death in real time. Each was followed by new all-time highs that made the previous peak look like a speed bump.

But here's the key that separates wealth builders from perpetual spectators: those who made life-changing wealth didn't invest their "fun money." They invested meaningful percentages of their net worth. The difference between investing $1,000 and $50,000 when Bitcoin was at $3,000 is the difference between a nice dinner and generational wealth.

When Bitcoin crashed to $3,800 during the March 2020 pandemic panic, everyone said it was going to zero. The world was ending. But understanding the J-curve means knowing that maximum pessimism creates maximum opportunity. Those who bet big when others were paralyzed by fear saw their positions multiply 25x as Bitcoin recovered to new highs.

Or take Ethereum's dramatic swings. Imagine buying heavily at $400, then watching it crash to $80—an 80% drawdown that would make most people physically ill. Instead of panic-selling, what if you bought more? Not $100 more. Tens of thousands more. Real money that represented months of savings or business profits. When Ethereum eventually hit $4,800, those who had bet lunch money made lunch money. Maybe they turned $500 into $6,000, enough for a vacation. Those who had bet big? They secured house down payment money. Life changing money. The kind that buys time freedom, which as we discussed in chapter 23, is the only real wealth.

This connects directly to the velocity principles from chapter 20. When you bet big during J-curves, you're not just making money; you're creating capital that can be deployed across DeFi strategies. That $50,000 Bitcoin position that becomes $500,000? Now you can borrow against it as we covered in chapter 17, provide liquidity with the borrowed funds per chapter 18, and generate yields that dwarf traditional employment income.

Every J-curve you navigate successfully compounds into the next. The first crypto J-curve teaches recognition of opportunity in chaos. The second teaches position sizing. The third teaches using ladder-out strategies from chapter 16 to actually capture gains instead of round-tripping them. By the fourth major cycle, you don't just survive J-curves; you hunt them.

This is what HODLers understand intuitively, as we explored in chapter 12. They're not just "holding and hoping." They're navigating a series of J-curves, each one strengthening their conviction, increasing their position size, and improving their execution. The weak hands who sell at the bottom of each J-curve transfer their wealth to those who understand the pattern.

The psychological transformation is even more valuable than the financial gains. Navigate one J-curve successfully, and you develop courage. Navigate two, and you develop pattern recognition. Navigate three, and you develop the unshakeable conviction that allows you to bet big when others are paralyzed by fear. You become someone who can handle 70% drawdowns without flinching because you've seen them reverse into 400% gains.

This ties directly to the risk management principles you'll read about in chapter 25. The Kelly Criterion would actually suggest massive positions during crypto J-curve bottoms. When Bitcoin is down 80% from all-time highs, historical data shows a 90%+ probability of eventual recovery to new highs. The math literally screams at you to bet big. But most people can't because they haven't developed the psychological fortitude through navigating previous J-curves.

Every J-curve also teaches you about impermanent loss in a broader sense, building on chapter 19. When your portfolio drops 70%, that's essentially impermanent loss if you don't sell (technically it's unrealized losses, but I'm trying to make a point). It only becomes permanent (realized) when you panic-sell at the bottom. Those who understand this aren't destroyed by drawdowns; they're energized by the opportunity to accumulate at discounts.

The DeFi strategies we explored in Part IV become even more powerful during J-curves. While your spot positions are down, you can be earning 50% APY by providing liquidity, as detailed in chapter 21. The yields you generate during the bear market become the capital for aggressive accumulation. Sophisticated investors live entirely off DeFi yields during bear markets while accumulating spot positions that will later multiply in value.

Also, note that the J-curve isn't just about price. It's about the entire ecosystem development. During the 2018 to 2020 crypto winter, prices were dead but DeFi was being built. Uniswap launched. Aave emerged. The infrastructure for the next boom was constructed while tourists had given up. Those who stayed engaged, learning and building during the J-curve, were perfectly positioned when the market turned. That's actually when I went all in on Cryptolabs Research. No one was building communities or creating YouTube content during that crypto winter, and so I did the only thing I know: I doubled down.

This is why understanding market cycles from chapter 11 combined with J-curve dynamics creates unstoppable wealth building. You know Bitcoin will lead the recovery. You know Ethereum will follow with higher beta. You know altseason will eventually arrive with life-changing gains. But you also know another J-curve waits after the euphoria. So you ladder out per chapter 16, preserve capital, and prepare to bet big on the next dip.

Consider the mathematical reality of someone who navigated just three J-curves successfully. First J-curve: $10,000 becomes $100,000. Second J-curve: $100,000 deployed at the bottom becomes $1,000,000. Third J-curve: $1,000,000 becomes $10,000,000. This isn't fantasy. This is the documented path of thousands of crypto millionaires who understood and embraced J-curves.

Every J-curve you navigate successfully doesn't just improve your circumstances; it fundamentally transforms who you are. You evolve from someone who fears volatility to someone who profits from it. From someone who needs external validation to someone with internal conviction. From someone who works for money to someone who makes money work at velocities traditional finance can't imagine.

The next time Bitcoin crashes 50%, you won't see disaster. You'll see the J-curve forming. You'll see the weak hands capitulating. You'll see the opportunity to deploy meaningful capital at discounts. And you'll act with the conviction that comes from understanding that every J-curve in crypto's history has led to new all-time highs.

The question isn't whether you'll encounter J-curves in crypto. You will, repeatedly. The question is whether you'll navigate them with lunch money or life-changing money. Whether you'll panic at the bottom or accumulate with conviction. Whether you'll emerge from each J-curve the same person or transformed into someone capable of building generational wealth.

The J-curve isn't something to endure. It's something to embrace, even seek out. Because on the other side of every J-curve isn't just financial gain. It's the evolution into someone who can navigate any challenge, capture any opportunity, and build wealth in any market condition.

What's Your J-Curve Moment?

Playing small in today's economy guarantees failure. Save $500 monthly for 20 years and inflation turns your $260,000 into barely enough for a house down payment. You'll work until 65 and retire poor.

Betting big means accepting temporary pain for exponential gain. Yes, you might fail and start over. But in this economy, you're starting over anyway when inflation destroys your savings or AI eliminates your job. At least betting big means failing forward with skills and experience that compound.

Small bets in a system designed to keep you small will never create freedom. The economy has changed. When inflation runs at 7% and wages grow at 2%, your only chance at financial freedom is betting big on yourself and embracing the J-curve completely.

That business idea you've been sitting on? Start building. That investment opportunity that scares you? Make it meaningful. That skill you want to develop? Go all in. In a world where playing it safe guarantees failure, the biggest risk you can take is not swinging for the fences when you step up to the plate.

25

Risk vs. Reward:
How Real Investors Think

Risk and reward aren't enemies in crypto; they're the twin engines that create life-changing returns. Understanding their relationship at a mathematical level separates the builders of generational wealth from those who never capture crypto's full potential.

The fundamental equation that governs all investing is beautifully simple: Expected Value = (Probability of Win × Size of Win) - (Probability of Loss × Size of Loss). Most traditional investors never calculate this because their boring 7% annual returns don't require it. But in crypto, where 20x returns are possible, mastering this equation literally pays millions.

The best opportunities in crypto offer asymmetric risk-reward where downside might be 20% but upside is 200%. That's the kind of math that creates millionaires.

Understanding Risk in Crypto Markets

Risk in crypto isn't something to fear; it's something to understand, manage, and profit from. The volatility that scares traditional investors is exactly what creates our opportunity. There are multiple risks in crypto:

Market risk means everything can drop 50% when Bitcoin corrects. But that's also why we can make 400% when it rallies. The same volatility that creates fear creates fortune for those who understand it.

Protocol risk exists at the smart contract level, which is why we stick with battle-tested platforms that have secured billions for years. Aave, Uniswap, and Compound have processed trillions in value with remarkably few failures. When you use established protocols, you're using infrastructure that's proven itself through years of attempted attacks that failed.

Liquidity risk teaches us to focus on quality over quantity. That micro-cap might promise 1000x, but if you can't sell it, those are just numbers on a screen. Blue-chip assets like Bitcoin and Ethereum have deep liquidity. You can move millions without moving the market. This liquidity ensures you can actually realize gains.

Regulatory risk is real but manageable. Governments have been "about to ban crypto" for fifteen years. Yet here we are with Bitcoin ETFs, institutional adoption, and countries making Bitcoin legal tender. Each regulatory scare that doesn't kill crypto makes it stronger. We're not operating in shadows; we're building the future of finance in broad daylight.

The Kelly Criterion

The Kelly Criterion isn't just theory; it's the mathematical foundation for optimal position sizing that maximizes long-term wealth. Discovered by John Kelly at Bell Labs in 1956, it was initially used to optimize signal transmission but quickly adopted by legendary investors like Warren Buffett and Ed Thorp. When applied correctly, it ensures you're betting enough to build wealth quickly but not so much that one bad trade wipes you out.

The formula itself is elegant: $f = (bp - q) / b$, where f is the fraction of your bankroll to bet, b is the odds received on the bet, p is the probability of winning, and q is the probability of losing. This mathematical precision removes emotion from position sizing, replacing gut feelings with calculated optimization.

Let's apply this to a real opportunity. You've identified a quality project through thorough research. Your analysis suggests a 60% chance of 3x returns (the project succeeds and price triples) and a 40% chance of 50% loss (the project fails or underperforms). Plugging into Kelly: $b = 2$ (you win 2x your bet for a 3x return), p = 0.60, q = 0.40. The calculation yields f = (2 × 0.60 - 0.40) / 2 = 0.40, suggesting you risk 40% of your crypto allocation.

But here's where practical wisdom meets mathematical theory. Full Kelly betting is notoriously aggressive and assumes perfect probability estimates. Since we're human and our probabilities are estimates, using fractional Kelly is prudent. Most successful investors use 25% to 50% of the Kelly suggestion. At 25% fractional Kelly, you'd risk 10% of your crypto allocation.

This is aggressive enough to build wealth but conservative enough to survive. Even if you're wrong and the project fails, you've lost 10% of your crypto allocation, not catastrophic. But if you're right, that 10% position triples, adding 20% to your portfolio value. Do this successfully several times and you're building serious wealth.

The beauty of Kelly betting in crypto is that our risk–reward ratios are much more favorable compared to traditional markets. Traditional markets might offer 20% upside with 20% downside, a 1:1 ratio that Kelly finds uninspiring. Crypto regularly offers 500% upside with 50% downside, a 10:1 ratio that makes Kelly calculations scream, "Bet big!" Even using conservative fractional Kelly, the math supports larger positions than you'd ever take in traditional markets.

Consider Bitcoin in March 2020 at $4,000. Historical data suggested 70% probability of recovery to previous highs ($20,000) within two years, a 5x return. Downside was perhaps 50% if crypto winter continued. Kelly would have suggested a massive position, and even fractional Kelly at 25% would have recommended a substantial allocation. Those who followed the math turned $20,000 into $100,000, or $100,000 into $500,000.

The Kelly Criterion also teaches a counterintuitive lesson: sometimes the optimal bet is zero. If your edge isn't clear, if the risk-reward isn't favorable, Kelly says don't bet. This discipline prevents the small losses that compound into large losses over time.

Building Your Risk-Optimized Portfolio

As we explored in chapter 5, asymmetric bets where you can lose 1x but gain 20x are the secret to crypto wealth. Now let's talk about structuring your entire portfolio to capture these opportunities while surviving inevitable drawdowns.

Risk parity isn't about equal weights but equal risk contribution. This naturally creates the optimal portfolio structure that balances stability with explosive upside potential. Your foundation should be at least 50% Bitcoin, providing the stability and consistent appreciation that anchors everything else. When altcoins crash 90%, Bitcoin might only drop 50%, and that relative stability matters for portfolio survival.

Layer on 30% Ethereum to capture smart contract innovation and DeFi growth. More volatile than Bitcoin but with higher upside, Ethereum offers the nearly perfect risk-reward balance for wealth building. Add 20% in blue-chip DeFi tokens like AAVE, UNI, and LINK that have proven themselves through multiple cycles, generating yield while appreciating. Finally, if you really want to have exposure to some moonshots, you can free up 5% of your portfolio (take a few points off Bitcoin, Ethereum, and/or your blue-chip holdings) and allocate it to your moonshots—those small bets on emerging projects that could 100x. Most will fail, but one winner pays for all losers and then creates generational wealth.

This structure ensures you capture massive upside while surviving drawdowns. But position sizing within this framework matters equally. Other than Bitcoin and Ethereum, no single position should exceed 15% of your crypto allocation because concentration risk is unnecessary when the whole market is growing. But positions below 1% are too small to matter when they hit. Find the sweet spot between meaningful exposure and survivable risk.

The Survival Strategy That Creates Millionaires

In crypto, survival doesn't mean avoiding risk; it means *taking calculated risks repeatedly while ensuring you can continue playing the game.* Every cycle you survive is another opportunity for 10x to 100x returns. The math is simple: if you can capture just one 10x per cycle while avoiding elimination, you'll build generational wealth.

Keeping dry powder isn't about fear; it's about opportunity. When markets crash 50%, having capital to deploy generates returns that dwarf any opportunity cost from holding some cash. The ability to buy when others are forced to sell is the most valuable option in crypto. This is why being smart with leverage matters so much. Leverage might double your gains, but it can eliminate you entirely. The unleveraged investor who survives every cycle and compounds returns beats the leveraged trader every time, even if the leveraged trader has higher returns in good times.

Risk management in crypto isn't about avoiding losses, either. It's about ensuring losses don't prevent you from capturing massive gains. When positions hit 50% gains, take profit. At 2x, take another 20%. At 3x and 5x, continue laddering out per the strategy from chapter 16. This ensures you realize gains while maintaining exposure to infinite upside, systematically converting paper gains into permanent wealth while keeping that final 20% as your moonshot position.

Diversification across strategies multiplies opportunities beyond just holding different assets. While your holdings appreciate, your DeFi positions generate yield. While yields compound, you're systematically accumulating more assets. Multiple strategies mean multiple ways to win, and more importantly, they smooth out returns during different market conditions. Time diversification matters even more than asset diversification. Buying consistently through all market conditions beats trying to time entries. The investor who buys monthly for four years beats the one trying to perfectly time the bottom—every single time.

Value at Risk and Stress-Testing Your Wealth

Value at Risk calculations are all about taking the maximum profitable risk *you can handle psychologically and financially.* A $10,000 DeFi position might have a 95% VaR of $3,000 over 30 days, meaning 95% of the time, you won't lose more than $3,000. More importantly, while your downside is statistically limited to that $3,000 loss most of the time, your upside remains unlimited.

If you can handle that $3,000 drawdown both financially and emotionally, you're positioned for the 10x moves that change lives. You're always calculating (and accepting) risk against the reward.

Feel free to stress-test your portfolio. Model what happens if Bitcoin drops 70%, if DeFi yields compress to 5%, if your moonshots go to zero. When you know your portfolio can survive these scenarios, you don't panic-sell the bottom. You've already accepted it, and you're ready to buy the opportunities. This preparation allowed smart investors to accumulate Bitcoin at $3,800 in March 2020 while others panicked. They had already mentally accepted the drawdown, so they could act rationally when it arrived.

The psychological component of risk management often matters more than the mathematical component. **You need to size positions so you can sleep at night, because tired, stressed investors make terrible decisions.** If a position keeps you awake worrying, it's too large regardless of what Kelly Criterion says. Find your personal maximum pain point and stay well below it. This ensures you can hold through volatility rather than panic-selling bottoms.

Master the Math, Build the Wealth

Understanding risk and reward at this level transforms you from nervous investor to confident wealth builder. You stop fearing volatility and start harvesting it. You stop avoiding risk and start optimizing it. You understand that in a market growing from $2 trillion to $20 trillion this decade, the biggest risk is not taking enough risk.

The investors building lasting wealth in crypto aren't avoiding risk; they're mastering it. They use mathematical frameworks like Kelly Criterion to size positions optimally. They structure portfolios to capture upside while surviving drawdowns. They take profits systematically while maintaining exposure to exponential gains. They understand that volatility is the price of opportunity, and they're willing to pay it. And most importantly, they're playing the long game. They're in it for the long haul. They know it's the future, and they're positioning themselves NOW for it.

The math doesn't lie: crypto's risk-reward ratio is the best opportunity in financial history. Master these principles, embrace calculated risk, and prepare for returns that transform your family's financial future forever.

26

Wealth Principles They
Don't Teach You In School

Wealth isn't about how much you earn. It's not about just how much you keep, either. The real wealth game is measured by how hard it works for you, and how long it lasts. The middle class focuses on income. *The wealthy focus on assets.* This fundamental difference in focus creates an ever-widening gap that compounds over generations.

The rich don't get richer through luck or conspiracy. They get richer through understanding principles of wealth that operate like laws of physics, consistent, predictable, and available to anyone who learns them. The poor and middle class stay stuck not because they lack opportunity (come on, it's 2025, the opportunities are literally endless), but because they've been programmed with beliefs about money that guarantee they'll never accumulate it.

School taught you to work for money. This chapter teaches you how money works. The difference between those two educations is the difference between lifetime employment and generational wealth.

What The Wealthy Know

The wealthy understand a simple equation that changes everything: **Wealth = Assets – Liabilities.** Not income minus expenses. Not salary minus bills. Assets minus liabilities. It's the fundamental distinction between staying broke and building wealth.

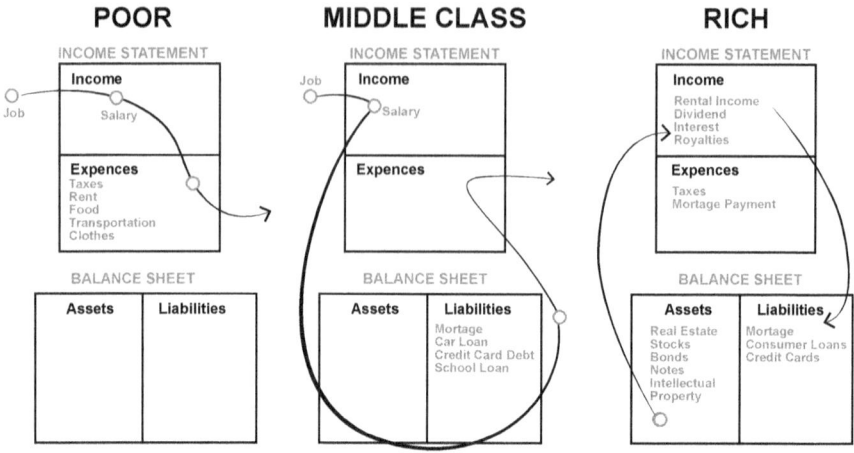

Look at these three balance sheets by Robert Kiyosaki, author of Rich Dad, Poor Dad. The one in the center shows the middle-class trap: income flows directly to expenses, leaving the balance sheet empty. Every month starts at zero. Work, earn, spend, repeat. The rat race visualized.

The right shows the wealthy framework: assets generate income that covers expenses first, then flows back to buy more assets. The balance sheet grows continuously. Money makes money. Assets buy assets. This is the system you're building.

Assets put money in your pocket without your active involvement. Rental properties generating rent. Stocks paying dividends. Crypto generating yield through DeFi. Businesses producing profit whether you show up or not. These assets work twenty-four hours a day, never call in sick, never quit, never ask for raises. They're employees that pay you instead of the other way around.

The middle class buys liabilities thinking they're assets, and this confusion keeps them trapped forever. The house you live in isn't an asset; it costs you money monthly through mortgage, maintenance, taxes, and insurance. The car you drive isn't an asset; it depreciates the moment you buy it while demanding constant feeding through gas, insurance, and repairs. The boat, the vacation home, the expensive toys, all liabilities disguised as success symbols that drain wealth rather than create it.

Watch what happens to the typical middle-class progression. They get a promotion and immediately increase their liabilities. Bigger house because they "deserve it." Nicer car because they can "afford the payment." Expensive vacation because they "earned it." Each increase in income triggers an equal or greater increase in liabilities. They're running faster on a treadmill going nowhere, wondering why they never get ahead despite making more money.

The wealthy operate in reverse. They buy assets first, lifestyle second. They understand that assets buy freedom, while liabilities without assets buy imprisonment. Every dollar spent on liabilities first is a dollar not acquiring assets. Every asset acquired is a soldier in your wealth army, fighting for your freedom around the clock.

I love cars, motorcycles, and anything with an engine. My garage looks like a dealership. But here's the crucial difference: my assets pay for my liabilities. My DeFi yields buy my toys. Crypto profits fund new adventures. Business income funds my lifestyle. The assets came first, the liabilities came from asset and investment income. This sequence matters more than the amounts. When your assets buy your liabilities, you can enjoy them without guilt or financial stress because they're not preventing wealth accumulation, they're a reward for it.

Kiyosaki's Cashflow Quadrant

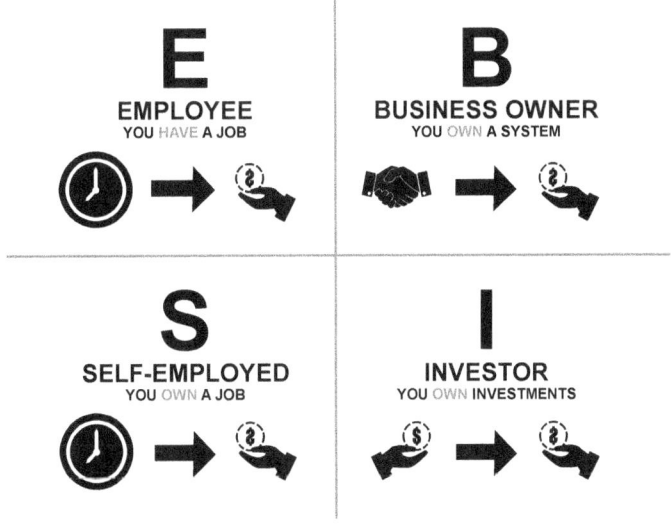

Robert Kiyosaki's Cashflow Quadrant reveals another truth the wealthy understand. The world divides into four groups:

E (Employee): Trading time for money. Limited by hours in a day. One income stream. Highest taxes. No leverage.

S (Self-Employed): Still trading time for money but at higher rates. If you stop, income stops. You own a job, not a business.

B (Business Owner): Systems and people generate money. Income continues without your presence. True leverage through others' time.

I (Investor): Money makes money. Complete separation of time from income. Lowest taxes. Maximum leverage.

The middle class lives on the left side (E and S), thinking they're progressing when they move from employee to self-employed. But they're still trading time for money. The wealthy live on the right side (B and I), where systems and capital generate income independent of their time.

Crypto accelerates your transition to the right side. DeFi positions make you an investor immediately. Building automated yield strategies makes you a business owner. You can jump from E to I in months, not decades. The traditional path required massive capital. Crypto requires only knowledge and conviction.

The Compound Effect and Velocity of Money

Einstein allegedly called compound interest the eighth wonder of the world. The principle remains the most powerful force in wealth building, yet most people never harness it because they don't understand how to combine it with velocity.

Compound growth isn't linear; it's exponential. Take $10,000 growing at 10% annually. After thirty years, it's $174,494. But the wealthy don't accept 10%. Through strategic investing and velocity optimization, they achieve 20% or higher returns. That same $10,000 at 20% for thirty years becomes $2.3 million.

The middle class interrupts compounding constantly without understanding the catastrophic cost. They cash out retirement accounts for "emergencies," sell investments for vacations, reset their compound curve to zero repeatedly. A $10,000 withdrawal after ten years doesn't just cost $10,000; it costs the $174,494 that money would have become.

But velocity is the multiplier most people miss entirely. I know we already discussed velocity in chapter 20, but it's worth repeating: the wealthy understand that money sitting still is dying money. They keep capital moving through productive assets at maximum velocity. In DeFi, this reaches speeds traditional finance can't imagine. The same capital earning yields, capturing arbitrage, and providing liquidity all in a single day. One dollar doing the work of ten dollars through velocity optimization.

This combination of uninterrupted compounding and maximum velocity is how the wealthy build fortunes while others struggle. They never break the compound curve, and they ensure every dollar works at maximum efficiency. Master both principles, and wealth becomes a mathematical certainty.

The Leverage Multiplication System

The wealthy understand that leverage isn't just about borrowing money; it's about multiplying every form of capital to create exponential rather than linear growth.

Financial leverage gets the most attention but is often misunderstood. The middle class fears all debt because they only know consumer debt that buys depreciating liabilities. The wealthy embrace productive debt that acquires appreciating assets. Borrowing at 4% to buy real estate yielding 10% isn't risky; it's mathematical arbitrage. Borrowing at 8% to invest in a business returning 30% isn't speculation; it's leverage optimization. The key is that the asset must generate more than the debt costs, creating positive leverage that multiplies wealth.

But the real power comes from stacking multiple forms of leverage simultaneously. Knowledge leverage happens through systems and processes. The wealthy don't repeat tasks; they systematize them once and benefit forever. A process that saves an hour daily saves 365 hours annually. Multiply that across an organization, and you've leveraged knowledge into massive efficiency. A YouTube video teaching a concept once can educate millions forever. That's infinite knowledge leverage.

Relationship leverage multiplies opportunities exponentially. Every relationship is potential access to deals, capital, knowledge, or other relationships. The wealthy invest in relationships like financial assets, understanding that one introduction can be worth millions. They join masterminds, boards, and investment clubs not for the immediate benefit but for the compound relationship value over time. One connection leads to five, which leads to twenty-five, which leads to deals you'd never see otherwise.

Time leverage through hiring is how the wealthy escape the hours-for-dollars trap. Every employee multiplies your productive capacity. A business with hundred employees has hundred times the potential output of a solo operation. But more importantly, it separates your income from your time. The business generates wealth whether you're working, sleeping, or traveling. This is the ultimate leverage, turning time from a constraint into an asset.

Technology leverage is the newest and most powerful form. A single app can serve millions of users with minimal additional cost. A DeFi protocol can process billions in transactions with the same code. The wealthy understand that technology doesn't just improve efficiency; it removes the relationship between effort and output entirely. One unit of effort can produce infinite output through technology leverage.

The Information Advantage

The tax code wasn't written for wage earners; it was written by and for asset owners. Understanding this architecture combined with information asymmetry is how the wealthy keep most of what they make while others give away nearly half.

Employment income gets taxed the heaviest globally. Whether you're in the US, the UK, Canada, or Australia, your paycheck gets hit before you see it. But investment income receives preferential treatment almost everywhere.

Capital gains, dividends, and business income all get better tax treatment than wages. The message is universal: the system rewards investing over working.

Business owners have flexibility employees don't. They deduct expenses before paying taxes while employees pay taxes before expenses. The same laptop, meal, or trip can be a deductible business expense or after-tax personal expense depending on your structure. The wealthy structure everything through businesses first, personal second.

But here's what matters more than specific tax rates. The wealthy don't focus on avoiding taxes; they focus on building assets so valuable that taxes become a small percentage of gains. When your DeFi position makes 200%, paying 20% or even 40% tax still leaves you with massive profits. The middle class obsesses over saving hundreds in taxes while the wealthy focus on making millions in gains.

In crypto, the tax advantage is even clearer. Hold for over a year in most jurisdictions, and you get long-term capital gains treatment. Use DeFi loans instead of selling, and you access liquidity without triggering taxable events. Stake and earn yield that compounds tax-deferred until you sell. The strategies that build wealth also optimize taxes naturally.

Information asymmetry becomes the real differentiator. The wealthy understand that information is the ultimate asset. Not public information everyone knows, but asymmetric information that creates advantage. They position themselves where valuable information flows naturally. Who you know determines what you know, and what you know determines what opportunities you see.

In crypto, information asymmetry is everything. Knowing about a protocol before launch, understanding a narrative before it spreads, recognizing opportunity before consensus forms. These asymmetries create fortunes. The wealthy don't wait for information to reach them; they position themselves at the source. They're in the Discord servers where developers discuss plans. They're in the Telegram groups where VCs share deal flow. They're in groups like the Underdog Investor Group where alpha flows and investors share their research. They're actively creating information asymmetry in their favor.

Breaking the Programming and Building Wealth

The middle class stays stuck because they're programmed with beliefs that guarantee poverty. These programs run unconsciously, sabotaging every attempt at wealth building. "Money doesn't grow on trees" programs a scarcity mindset. "Money is the root of all evil" programs guilt about accumulation. "We can't afford it" programs limitation thinking. "Rich people are greedy" programs rejection of wealth. These beliefs, installed in childhood, operate like malware in your financial operating system.

The wealthy program different beliefs that create different outcomes. "Money is a tool for freedom and impact." … "Value creation generates wealth naturally." … "Assets buy time and choice." … "We choose how to allocate capital strategically." They understand that beliefs drive behaviors, behaviors drive results, and results reinforce beliefs. It's either a virtuous or vicious cycle depending on your programming.

Reprogramming requires both mental and practical work. Every time you think, "I can't afford it," replace that thought with, "How can I create the value to afford it?" Every time you think, "That's too risky," ask, "How can I minimize the risk while capturing the upside?" But reprogramming goes beyond affirmations to action. You must act wealthy before becoming wealthy. Make decisions from abundance, not scarcity. Invest in yourself before seeing returns. Think in assets, not expenses. Buy assets that appreciate, not liabilities that depreciate.

Start by shifting focus from income to net worth. Calculate your true net worth monthly: assets minus liabilities. Make increasing it your primary financial metric, not your salary. Build your first income-generating asset immediately. In crypto, this might be a DeFi position earning yield. Start with $100 if that's all you have. One asset becomes two becomes ten becomes freedom. The amount matters less than starting the accumulation process.

Protect compound growth religiously. Never interrupt compounding without extreme justification. Build emergency funds so investments never get touched. Think in decades, not years. Every withdrawal resets your compound curve to zero. Every asset sold is future wealth destroyed. Borrow against assets rather than selling them. Let compound interest work its magic undisturbed.

The Wealth Revolution in Real Time

These principles aren't theory; they're the operating system the wealthy use to build and maintain fortune. They work regardless of starting point, but crypto accelerates them dramatically. Assets can be accumulated fractionally, starting with dollars instead of thousands. Compound growth happens per block, every few seconds, instead of annually. Leverage is programmable through smart contracts. Velocity reaches speeds impossible in traditional finance. The same principles that took generations now work in years.

But principles without action are just philosophy. The wealthy build while others read about wealth. They implement while others plan. They compound while others consume. Information without implementation is entertainment, not education.

You now understand why the rich get richer. Not through conspiracy, but through principles. Not through luck, but through systems. These principles have worked for centuries and will work for centuries more. The question isn't whether these principles work; the question is whether you'll apply them.

The gap between wealthy and everyone else is widening along lines of understanding, not birthright. Anyone can learn these principles. Anyone can apply them. But most won't. They'll return to trading time for money, buying liabilities thinking they're assets, interrupting compounding for consumption, avoiding leverage from fear, accepting high taxes from ignorance.

You have a choice. Apply these principles and join the wealth-building minority, or ignore them and remain in the struggling majority. Start acquiring assets today. Protect compounding religiously. Optimize velocity relentlessly. Leverage every form of capital. Structure for tax efficiency. Build information asymmetry. The principles don't care about your choice. They'll continue operating regardless, making the rich richer and keeping the poor poor.

Which side will you be on?

See Ya Out There!

Right now, millions of people are using the strategies in this book to build wealth. They're earning 50% APY while others research endlessly without acting. They're accumulating Bitcoin while many still debate timing. They're providing liquidity and earning fees while others wait for certainty that never comes. The revolution isn't coming. *It's here*, happening in real time, and every day of hesitation is opportunity cost accumulating.

With that said, thank you for reading this book and trusting me with your time. Thank you for having the courage to question a system that's been eroding your wealth through inflation, fees, and restricted access. But most importantly, thank you for joining us in building the replacement.

Because that's what we're doing here. We're not just escaping the traditional financial system. We're making it obsolete. Every Bitcoin purchased is a vote against currency debasement. Every DeFi transaction proves banks are unnecessary middlemen. Every smart contract interaction demonstrates that code is more trustworthy than institutions. We're not protesters with signs; we're revolutionaries with capital, building the future one transaction at a time.

This isn't just about personal wealth, though everyone deserves to build wealth after years of systematic value extraction. This is about fundamentally restructuring how humanity coordinates value. For the first time in history, we have money that can't be printed at will, financial services that can't discriminate based on geography, and economic infrastructure that operates without permission from gatekeepers who profit from exclusion.

So welcome to the family. And I mean that literally. When you buy your first Bitcoin, you join millions worldwide who've declared independence from financial tyranny. You strengthen a network that grows more powerful with every participant. Every dollar invested weakens the old system and strengthens the new one. You're not just an investor; you're a revolutionary, and revolutions are won by communities, not individuals.

Imagine a world where sending money is as easy as sending a text, where loans are instant and based on collateral rather than credit scores, where savings actually grow rather than melt, where financial services are available 24/7/365 to anyone with internet access. We're not imagining this world. We're building it, block by block, transaction by transaction, one new crypto holder at a time.

In ten years, traditional banking will seem as outdated as mailing checks. In twenty years, the idea that governments could print money at will will seem as primitive as bloodletting. This transformation isn't a possibility; it's an inevitability. The only question is whether you'll help build it or watch others create the greatest wealth transfer in human history.

Your Next Steps

Right now, if you haven't already, go open an account on Coinbase, Kraken, or Binance. Buy $100 of Bitcoin. Then add some Ethereum. Don't overthink it. The perfect entry doesn't exist; entering does. While your account verifies, subscribe to CryptoLabs Research on YouTube (https://youtube.com/@cryptolabsresearch). Over 1,400 videos packed with value are waiting for you. Not hype, not hopium. Actual strategies from investors who escaped wage slavery through crypto.

Follow **@lucasrubix** on Instagram for daily insights and direct access to ask questions.

Bookmark **DeFiBuddy.io** for finding opportunities, calculating returns, and tracking your portfolio. No signup required, just a free and powerful tool for monitoring your journey.

Take our free DeFi University course at www.TheDeFiUniversity.com. Over 10,000 students have used it to master DeFi basics. Every protocol, every strategy, explained in plain English. The education that costs nothing but could make you millions. You'll have access to live calls once or twice a month to ask questions and see portfolios being built in real time.

When you're ready to level up faster, come join the **Underdog Investor Group** (UIG), where thousands of investors share strategies, support each other through volatility, and capture opportunities together. Some started with $1,000 and now manage six figures, and others have 7-figure portfolios and beyond. All underdogs, all winning. You'll have access to a team of researchers, coaches, and professional investors to help guide you through this wild world of crypto. Learn more about the Underdog Investment Group at www.CryptoLabsResearch.com.

Free Tools:

- CryptoLabs Research (YouTube): https://youtube.com/@cryptolabsresearch
- The DeFi University: www.TheDeFiUniversity.com
- DeFiBuddy.io: Portfolio tracking and market research
- @lucasrubix (Instagram): DM me your questions

Work With Us:

- We run the Underdog Investor Group (our investor community) and the DeFi Fast Track Program (our Mastermind for serious investors). If you'd like to join a community of serious investors then hop on over to www.CryptoLabsResearch.com to learn more.

Remember:

The traditional system wants you poor and dependent. We're building something different. Where anyone can be their own bank, where an underdog from anywhere can access a level of opportunity formerly limited to Wall Street. This isn't just about money. It's about reclaiming sovereignty over your financial life and proving the underdog can win when the playing field is level.

The market doesn't wait. Opportunity doesn't pause. The revolution continues with or without you.

Welcome to the revolution. We've been waiting for you. Stop reading. Start building. Your future self will thank you.

Thank you for reading *Crypto Wealth Without Wall Street*. See you on You-Tube, Instagram, in DeFi University, and in the Underdog Investor Group!

—Lucas Rubix

About the Author

Lucas Rubix is the founder of CryptoLabs Research and The Underdog Investor Group, a research and education platform that have reached hundreds of thousands of people around the world and helped more than 5,000 investors navigate the rapidly evolving world of crypto and DeFi.

His journey began far from the world of finance. Working long shifts on oil rigs, trading time for money, and chasing someone else's definition of success. Through years of study, risk, and relentless execution, Lucas built multiple seven-figure businesses and achieved financial independence by mastering asymmetric investing and the principles of wealth creation beyond traditional systems.

Today, he's known for bridging practical investing with mindset and personal mastery. His mission is simple: to help others build real financial freedom, beat the banks and Wall Street at their own game, and live with purpose, sovereignty, and abundance.

www.ingramcontent.com/pod-product-compliance
Lightning Source LLC
Chambersburg PA
CBHW070910130626
46555CB00001B/83